St. Louis Community College

Forest Park
Florissant Valley
Meramec

Instructional Resources
St. Louis, Missouri

Jazz Man's Journey

A Biography of Ellis Louis Marsalis Jr.

D. Antoinette Handy

The Scarecrow Press, Inc.
Lanham, Maryland, and London
1999

SCARECROW PRESS, INC.

Published in the United States of America
by Scarecrow Press, Inc.
4720 Boston Way
Lanham, Maryland 20706
http://www.scarecrowpress.com

4 Pleydell Gardens, Folkestone
Kent CT20 2DN, England

British Library Cataloguing in Publication Information Available

Library of Congress Cataloging-in-Publication Data

Handy, D. Antoinette, 1930–
     Jazz man's journey : a biography of Ellis Louis Marsalis Jr. / by
D. Antoinette Handy.
        p.   cm.
     ISBN 1-57886-006-7 (cloth : alk. paper)
     1. Marsalis, Ellis.   2. Pianists—United States Biography.   3. Jazz
musicians—United States Biography.   I. Title.
ML417.M295H36   1999   99-16849
[B]   CIP

⊗™ The paper used in this publication meets the minimum requirements of
American National Standard for Information Sciences—Permanence of Paper for
Printed Library Materials, ANSI/NISO Z39.48–1992. Manufactured in the
United States of America.

This work is dedicated to
William Talbot Handy Jr., a United Methodist Church
bishop, a New Orleanian, a jazz devotee, and my recently
deceased brother (1924–1998).

Additional Photo Credits

Contents

Whereas this great American musical art form has not yet been properly recognized nor accorded the institutional status commensurate with its value and importance;

Whereas it is important for the youth of America to recognize and understand jazz as a significant part of their cultural and intellectual heritage;

Whereas in as much as there exists no effective national infrastructure to support and preserve jazz;

Whereas documentation and archival support required by such a great art form has yet to be systematically applied to the jazz field; and

Whereas it is in the best interest of the national welfare and all of our citizens to preserve and celebrate this unique art form: Now, therefore, be it resolved by the House of Representatives (the Senate concurring) that it is the sense of the Congress that jazz is hereby designated as a rare and valuable national American treasure to which we should devote our attention, support, and resources to make certain it is preserved, understood, and promulgated.

Passed the House of Representatives September 23, 1987
Passed the Senate December 4, 1987
Authored by Congressman John Conyers Jr., D—1st District, Michigan

New Orleans is a sound . . .
    A sound resulting from a long history of sounds.
    Original, Creative, Exciting, Happy, Sensual Sounds.

New Orleans is a place . . .
    A place that is alive! and lives for the music . . . for its sound.
    A place where the music lives in the people!

New Orleans is people . . .
    People who groove daily and nightly. People who's [sic] ordinary activities (walking and talking) have a groove that identifies them as New Orleanians!!

Harold R. Battiste Jr.

Preface

As early as 1982, I was convinced that there was a need for collective coverage of the Marsalis family, with emphasis on the father. The general public, as well as those involved in the music business, needed to understand where it all came from—the source. As Ellis III (third of six Marsalis boys, computer consultant, and Baltimore resident) stated to the author,

> I become irritated when people say, "Your father is 'cashing in' on the success of Wynton and Branford." I have to correct them. The old man's been doing his thing for a long time. High standards always; he's been very consistent. There's been no "cashing in." He's been playing forever. As children, we'd go to gigs with him. There weren't many in the audience. But it didn't bother him. He plays what he plays and is not fazed by what others do.[1]

Village Voice journalist Gary Giddins wrote, "A veteran New Orleans-based pianist *who sprang to the fore on the coattails of his amazing brood*" (emphasis added) in announcing a New York City club date.[2] *New York Times* music critic Peter Watrous, reviewing an Ellis Marsalis performance, wrote, "*[H]e basked in obscurity until the fame of his children brought him attention*" (emphasis added).[3] The editors of *All Music Guide to Jazz* wrote, "It is a bit ironic that Ellis Marsalis had to wait for sons Wynton and Branford to get famous before he was able to record on a regular basis, but Ellis has finally received his long overdue recognition."[4] These questions arise: To what extent are these statements "the gospel truth"? What are these writers suggesting? How valid are their points of view?

I returned to New Orleans (my hometown) in the fall of 1982 for an extended period, to assist with the care of my ailing father. During this time, I came to know Ellis as a superb pianist, composer, master teacher, musical philosopher, and beautiful human being. In addition, the name "Marsalis" was still in my memory, since the most popular gas station frequented by blacks in the early 1940s was an Esso (now Exxon) service station where my father purchased his gas. The manager was Ellis Marsalis Sr.

When I launched into the writing of this book, Branford and Wynton were regulars in the national and international press. Ellis Jr. was likewise acquiring more recognition both within New Orleans and outside of the city, as a performer, composer, and educator. He had been a frequent panelist at the National Endowment for the Arts[5] and served as an on-site evaluator for the agency. In 1990, he was elected vice president of the International Association of Jazz Educators (IAJE) and served on the Southern Arts Federation's board of directors.

I approached Ellis Jr. with a biography idea. I had completed several collective biographies and felt fully capable of tackling such a task. Then, too, Ellis was the ideal subject for me to deal with as my first "noncollective" biography. His reaction was always, "Fine with me, but you should confer with Dolores," his wife of thirty-six years and mother of his six sons. Finally approaching Dolores Marsalis, I made the mistake of saying to her, "I would like to take an in-depth look at the 'Marsalis Mystique.' I wish to better understand the phenomenon and assist others in doing the same." Use of the term "mystique" was a mistake. Dolores found it offensive and responded, "There is no mystery about the Marsalis family. My family happens to have some talent and they all work very hard. But that's no mystery."[6] After some personal analysis of our discussion, I determined that she was absolutely correct and abandoned the "family biography" idea. Dolores was kept apprised of the project and without her full agreement with the selected concept, the project would not be undertaken.

I returned to Jackson, Mississippi (less than three hours from New Orleans), in 1993. This had been home base for my academic years 1964–1966. In early 1995, I accepted an invitation to speak at Loyola University College of Music and to have lunch with Dr. David Swanzy (Dean) and Ellis Marsalis Jr. Swanzy was well aware of my desire as it related to the Marsalis family and was very familiar with Ellis, a master of music education graduate of Loyola. Swanzy had spent three months assisting me in Washington, D.C., in 1990. I had only recently been appointed director of the music program at the National Endowment for the Arts (after having arrived as assistant director). I have since learned that Ellis Jr. was one of several individuals who recommended me to the agency.

It was Swanzy who proposed the idea of a sole biography on Ellis, bringing in the family where appropriate. Ellis Louis Marsalis Jr. consented for me to be his biographer. Research was resumed and writing was launched.

Acknowledgments

There are many people to thank for their assistance with this project. Uppermost is Ellis's wife Dolores Marsalis; sons Wynton, Ellis III, Delfeayo, and Jason; father Ellis Sr.; and sister Yvette. A very special thank you to Dr. Lorraine Wilson, a personal friend of Ellis and Dolores, as well as mine; Jeanette Jennings, a member of Tulane University's social work faculty; Arneida Houston, reading and evalution specialist, Meharry Medical College; newspapermen Clarke Bustard (*Richmond Times Dispatch / Richmond News Leader*) and Lolis Elie (*New Orleans Times-Picayune*); Luana Clayton, retired professor of English (Jackson State University); and Corbie L. Johnson, secretary for the department of jazz studies, University of New Orleans. Needless to say, I have a tremendous debt to repay Ellis Marsalis Jr., for all of his splendid cooperation and for sharing so many details of his life with me, and with you the reader. I launch repayment with that which follows.

Foreword

Superb artist–musician, master teacher, loving husband, nurturing father, perfect gentleman, philosopher, proactive citizen, quintessential American: These are just a few ways to describe Ellis Marsalis, and Antoinette Handy suggests these and other characteristics to portray him in this fine biography.

Actually, I knew something of this special nature of Ellis Marsalis as a teacher, musician, and father even before I had the opportunity to read the first draft of this book. I have lived in New Orleans for the past twenty years, and no one living in New Orleans during that time could miss Ellis's presence in our city. His musical output as a performer has been immense and wonderful, and his reputation as a master teacher continues to grow and mature. And while the importance of a nurturing father may not be fully credited, almost everyone knows of the professional successes of his sons.

I arrived a bit late in New Orleans in the 1970s to observe the musically formative years of Branford, but I was fortunate to see, from a close distance, the meteoric evolution of Wynton's musical genius. As dean of the Loyola College of Music in the late 1970s, I watched Ellis make the weekly drop-offs at the front door of the music school, bringing his talented son for lessons with our trumpet teacher, George Jansen. And I listened, almost as often, to the excitement of Mr. Jansen as he expressed obvious pride in the growing accomplishments of his prize student.[*]

Lately, I have renewed my admiration of Ellis Marsalis as a nurturing father. His youngest son, Jason, has been with us as a music major at Loyola,

---

[*] Though no reference is made by Wynton to any of his private instructors, it appears to be appropriate to write something more about George Jansen. A member of the New Orleans Philharmonic in the late 1940s, he was Wynton's instructor during his last two years in high school. He had a stroke, which prevented him from playing, but he continued to teach until his death. A member of the Loyola University faculty, he was also the school's band director. [Footnote written by author]

and I see the low-key guidance from father Marsalis that is in the process of shaping another fine musician and young gentleman. Actually, Jason is already an accomplished musician, but it is clear to me that his father is guiding him toward the breadth, discipline, and maturation that may be gained from a structured educational environment. Jason has told me that his father neither forces opinions nor demands actions; instead, he says, Ellis points out alternatives and suggests opportunities to consider. This nurturing father is, to Jason, a wonderful teacher, first and foremost. It is clear that he respects his father as a superb artist, but it is Marsalis the teacher who had a profound effect on him.

When my friend, Antoinette Handy, first told me she wanted to write the biography of Ellis Marsalis, I was not surprised. She has written other fine books, including *Black Conductors* (1995). I was given an advance copy to read and was impressed with her ability to present factual information in an appealing as well as informative way.

I thought that her writing the biography of Ellis Marsalis was so important that I encouraged and, when needed, occasionally facilitated meetings with Ellis during several of her trips to New Orleans from Jackson, Mississippi. I can account for the fact that this was a labor of love by Antoinette, whose enthusiasm for writing an appropriate tribute to someone she so much admired was matched only by her desire to be as thorough and as factual as possible.

During one of her early visits to New Orleans, she asked for my opinion about some aspect in her writing, the particulars of which I have since forgotten. But I do remember my response and, in turn, her favorable reply.

"Let me write the foreword for your book," I volunteered, more as a way to express my hearty endorsement of her work than to gain an obviously favorable position within the covers of her book. It was also a logical desire that I had expressed, since I not only had known Ellis Marsalis for years but also had the very highest respect for him. His strength as an artist and his reputation as the father of world-class artists were only the tip of the iceberg; Antoinette, I knew, would dig much deeper.

And she did.

David Swanzy, Dean Emeritus
College of Music, Loyola University
New Orleans, Louisiana

The Making of New Orleans's Resident Genius, Ellis Marsalis Jr.

$\mathcal{J}$azz burst out of New Orleans and traveled up the river to a welcoming world. Now the music has come back home, helped no doubt by the early 1960s opening of Preservation Hall in the French Quarter. There were homebound Preservation Hall bands and traveling ones. It has been suggested that much is assumptive, since jazz never really left. Ellis Louis Marsalis Jr. is a true New Orleanian and is without a doubt the city's resident genius. Out of the city for brief periods, he always returned to home base.

One of the principal transporters of the music out of New Orleans from an earlier period was trumpeter Louis Armstrong (along with Sidney Bechet, King Oliver, Jelly Roll Morton, George Lewis, and Danny Barker). In later years, however, Armstrong wrote that maybe he should have remained in the Crescent City.[1]

New Orleans has long been recognized for its easy living, hospitality, food, and jazz. Since the early 1980s, it has become known as the city that gave the world the phenomenal Marsalis family.

The most familiar Marsalis names are those of Wynton and Branford. Of course the name Ellis should be added to the list. Richard Cook and Brian Morton designated father Ellis as founder of the Marsalis dynasty. "[No] mean player himself, one can hear where Wynton got his even-handed delineation of melody from and where Branford's aristocratic elegance of line is rooted."[2]

Father Ellis and mother Dolores are the proud parents of six sons, three of whom are outstanding musicians on an international scale (the youngest is known on a national scale, though approaching internationalism). The fourth child, Delfeayo, a more than adequate trombonist, has distinguished himself as a record producer, composer, and gifted writer. Performing on a national scale (approaching internationalism) is drummer Jason, a percussion major at Loyola University (New Orleans). Chances are that Jason will terminate his formal study after three years.[3] Ellis III (third child) is a computer consultant. Mboya, the fifth child, was diagnosed as autistic at age two. Born October 1, 1970, Mboya is their very special child. According to Dolores, "He makes the Marsalis family what it is."

The Marsalises were included in the 30th Anniversary Issue of *New Orleans*. The comment read, "If New Orleans's best gift to 20th century music was jazz, then New Orleans's best gift to 20th century music might be the entire Marsalis family."[4] Often designated as "the first family of jazz," the Marsalises provide justification for such a proclamation, with emphasis on pianist/composer/educator Ellis Marsalis.

Ellis Louis Marsalis Jr.—the subject of this book—was born November 14, 1934, to Ellis Louis Marsalis Sr. and Florence Marie Robertson. Two years later, sister Yvette Robertson Marsalis was born. The family lived in a duplex (on the top floor) at 1303 South Telemachus Street. "The lady who we rented from, Thelma Forte, became a good friend of my mother's. The house was in a section of New Orleans known as Gert Town."

Of the Gert Town years, Ellis recalled:

Mrs. Thelma Forte had a son named Jack, who was several years older than I was. I always believed that mother wanted me to be like Jack, whose ambition was to go into medicine. He became a dentist. I was impressed that he attended Gilbert Academy, a private black high school, and played alto saxophone. I was impressed also with his Gilbert Academy band uniform.

Another kid in the neighborhood, around my age, was named Alexander Dunbar. He too played alto saxophone, but was studying at the Xavier University Junior School of Music. With this environment, I was getting more and more interested in music.[5]

As a New Orleanian, I felt that I should have known more about Gert Town. Though I had heard the name, I assumed that it was from a distant past. I got some clarification when I read New Orleans journalist/radio commentator/record producer Kalamu ya Salaam's article, "Our Music Is No Accident," published in *The New Orleans Tribune*. Wrote Salaam,

Jazz was born on a sun day. Jazz was simply Congo Square, Part II, the African-American extension of the African root. Prior to the emancipation, our music happened in Congo Square, out around where the Municipal Auditorium and Armstrong Park are today. At the turn of the century, it was Lincoln Park—Lincoln Park, uptown New Orleans, off of Carrollton Avenue, a corner of the Black neighborhood now known as Gert Town.[6]

I also learned that Gert Town is not terribly far from the area where Marsalis Jr. and his family currently live (Pigeon Town).

During the course of a 1997 interview, Ellis Sr. indicated that Ellis Jr. was "always musically inclined and was very dutiful in what he wanted to do. I am told that as a teacher, he is tough." This of course explains for me why his students produce the way they do. I inquired of Ellis Sr. his assessment of Ellis and Dolores's children and their many accomplishments. His response: "I am very proud of them. They've accomplished a lot from the standpoint of music."[7]

Born 1908 in Amite County (Mississippi), at age 90 Ellis Sr. is a charming individual, in manner, appearance, and intellect, with quite a sense of humor. Some might refer to his style as "classic." Ellis Jr. is a replica of his father, simply a few years younger. The father says that he doesn't get out much now, except to take his walks and occasionally go to Sunday service. Something different was his appearance at grandson Delfeayo's 1997 wedding.

Florence Marie Robertson Marsalis, Ellis's mother, was born in 1907, in New Roads, Louisiana. She was her husband's helpmate as much as he would permit. After a lengthy illness (cancer), Mrs. Marsalis passed in 1973, at age 67. Though born in New Roads, Florence Marsalis was educated in New Orleans. She and her husband owned and operated a motel, the Marsalis Mansion. Her involvements lasted for twenty-nine years. Mrs. Marsalis held membership in the Music Lovers Guild, the Friendly Group Social and Pleasure Club, National Business League, and the Nationwide Hotel and Motel Association. Despite her many memberships and affiliations, however, her first commitments were to her family.

Much information on Ellis Jr.'s early years was provided by his sister Yvette. She was interviewed in 1997, on the same day that I conversed with Ellis Sr. She resides with her father and cares for him. Yvette indicated that Ellis was quite sickly as a child (a condition he has since outgrown) and hence was pampered (particularly by their mother). According to Ellis, their mother was overprotective of both of them.

Youth conflicts were common; but Ellis and Yvette were discouraged from fighting back, even if someone else struck the first blow. Their mother also discouraged them from playing with kids in the neighborhood, "though we could occasionally invite kids to our house."

Musically, Ellis was discouraged rather than encouraged. His parents felt that music was too risky. A degree in business would be much more appropriate and something to fall back on. Dillard University's music faculty advised that he should go into music education so that he could teach.

Someone once inquired of him, "What do you want to do?" He responded, "I want to be a musician." Then came, "But you can't make any money being a musician."

Yvette was very fond of her older brother. In her opinion, they survived because of him. "I was always trying to please Ellis. He was not interested in business, as our father had hoped."[8]

Ellis relayed the following information regarding his family to jazz journalist Leonard Feather:

> My father was always in business; he was self-supporting, and never had to take a porter's job. My mother never had to worry much about finances, though at one time she did go to work as a maid for a white doctor [before she married Ellis Sr.], and I suspect that a lot of the things she observed in that family influenced how she wanted to raise her children. She sent my sister and me to Xavier University Junior School of Music. My mother thought that this was what people did with their children—music and dance lessons; this was what a cultured family did.[9]

He started school at Rudolph T. Danneel when he was four years old.

> Starting early was nothing unusual for black kids. The white school board did not care much about what happened in our neighborhoods or our schools. One thing I remember about this school; it was a common practice in some classes, towards the end of the day, to encourage some students to tell stories. There was usually one kid in class who was good at storytelling. The class would ask that he or she be allowed to do it. My forte was spelling. I think my successes in spelling were primarily due to my being able to hear the sound of the words much as one would hear music intervals.[10]

Ellis and his family moved from Gert Town to the Shrewsbury area in the neighboring parish of Jefferson when he was around ten years old. Ellis Sr. purchased a house that had been the property of a popular white judge, which irritated many neighbors, both black and white. The house was on a corner lot facing River Road and Shrewsbury Road, where the streets were gravel from the levee to the highway. This being very rural, a lot of farming took place.

> Yvette and I were enrolled in the local black public school, which was about a six or eight block walk from where we lived. My class was divided into two grade levels. The sixth grade was on one side of the room and seventh grade on the other, both of which the one instructor taught simultaneously. The building was a three room wooden frame building, with an outhouse in the

back. For the eighth grade, students had to go to a school in Kenner, Louisiana, a small town about five or six miles north of Shrewsbury, or find another school.

My father was, at the time, continuing to manage a service station and decided to use his land to raise farm animals. Though the lot was not very large, we were raising chickens, ducks, a Jersey, a Holstein cow, and some hogs. I tried, with little success, to milk the Jersey cow, but could never get the milk to flow from the teats. . . . The barn would attract flies and the Jersey would fan them with her tail and consistently hit me in the head.

For a solid two years (ca. ages 10–12), I was responsible for killing and cleaning chickens for the family meals, collecting eggs from the nest in the morning and cleaning trays beneath the baby chicks. We also had mulberry, tangerine, persimmon, fig and plantain trees.

Yvette would take the persimmons to school and sell them. Mother would occasionally make mulberry pies. The animal kingdom was no more after 1946.[11]

Ellis Jr. tells us that a passing truck driver suggested in conversation with his father that he build a motel on the land. This he did, using the barn that housed the cows for conversion into the first five motel rooms. Over the next fifteen years, thirty rooms were added to the initial five. This is what became the Marsalis Mansion. Having persuaded his father to allow him to house a night club at the motel, with Ellis Jr. serving as proprietor, it took the pianist approximately six months (1962–1963) to realize that indeed, "business was not his thing." But artistically, Music Haven was a total success.

Before leaving Gert Town, Ellis had become enthralled with the sound of the clarinet. He begged his mother to purchase one, and she bought a new King model clarinet from Werlein's Music Store (the city's largest). He began studying at the Xavier University Junior School of Music. His teacher was Bernice Blache, a music major at the university. In a group class, it was a while before the instructor discovered that Ellis was not reading the music. "My good ears carried me over as long as they could. When the instructor began to give me some special attention, growth was fast." The following year, Ellis was given private lessons by one of the university's nuns. Fear of the sister caused him to miss his first two lessons. Before long, however, he was good enough to make the orchestra.

There was a violinist who, seated at the piano, taught Ellis three chords. "I played these three chords while he improvised above. The person who assisted was named Edward Frank, someone who I would encounter in later years."[12]

Following Danneel Elementary, Ellis entered Shrewsbury School, then F. P. Richard (where he met clarinetist Alvin Batiste), then Gilbert Academy, which he entered as a high school freshman. At F. P. Richard, he encountered his most fascinating study, a class in English literature that covered Countee Cullen, Langston Hughes, James Weldon Johnson, Claude McKay, and Paul Laurence Dunbar, as well as other black literary giants. This course he loved.

"My mother was told by a nun that because she sent me to an 'atheist' school, I could no longer attend Xavier University's Junior School of Music. I was enrolled then at Gilbert Academy (January 1948), which closed the following year. My parents then enrolled me at McDonogh #35. After three weeks, I was kicked out." He was then enrolled at Gaudet High School, an Episcopal school, from which he received his high school diploma.

One experience from Gilbert Academy is worthy of recall. Shortly after entering:

> I heard a rehearsal of the Swing Band and immediately wanted to join. The arrangements were primarily stock (i.e., arrangements that could be purchased from the local downtown music store). . .
>
> I had learned tenor saxophonist Red Prysock's hit recording called "Blues for the Red Boy.". . . This made me somewhat of a hero on tenor saxophone. The last year that Gilbert was opened some of us began talking about getting a band together. The Groovy Boys was born. Our primary engagements were dances at the African American YWCA. Our pianist, Roger Dickerson, brought to a rehearsal a request from his piano teacher, Mrs. Panell, for the group to play for a party for her students. The teacher "passed the hat" and collected $1.50 each.
>
> This was the beginning of our play for pay groups. We eventually charged $5.00 per man.[13]

While on the subject of his early training, it should be mentioned that Ellis received his first jazz lesson from Harold Battiste, currently Ellis's coworker at the University of New Orleans. Harold was then a senior at Dillard University.

> We were in the band room one day and he said, "Hey man, play me a C7 chord." I said, "What is that?" So he went to the blackboard and constructed some chord symbols. That was the first formal jazz lesson I ever had. There was no school for one to go to if he or she was seeking jazz education.[14]

While in his mid-teens, Ellis studied piano privately with Geneva Handy Rhone (Southall). The year was 1950. Sister Yvette studied with the same teacher. An April 10, 1950, class recital program featured Ellis and Yvette in the early intermediate category. Their assigned pieces were "Gypsy Lament" (DeLoone)—Yvette Marsalis, "Valse Charlene" (Rasbach)—Ellis Marsalis, and "Qui Vive" (Duet) (Ganz)—Ellis and Yvette Marsalis.

The most memorable teacher/student experience—private study with concert pianist Jean Coston Maloney—lasted for one year (1950–1951). According to Ellis:

> At one lesson, she stopped me and told me to play some jazz. After about eight measures, she said, "Wait a minute, stop. Hold your hands in the correct position, sit up at the piano, and start again." And a lightbulb went off. I had never transferred anything that I was doing in classical to what I was doing when I was trying to play jazz. So I became aware of using proper techniques of playing the instrument.[15]

Ellis entered Dillard University in 1951 (Yvette entered two years later), majoring in music. His plans were to continue the lessons, upon graduation, with Maloney. He was saddened to learn four years later that she had departed from the city. Ellis's first instrument was the clarinet (his college major), but by high school the tenor saxophone was the thing. Fortunately someone had the vision to encourage piano study at the same time. At Dillard University, his instructors were Dr. Melville Bryant and Mr. David Buttolph, clarinet; and Drs. Philip Rice and Ralph Simpson, piano. Upon college entrance, "I was two and a half months shy of my seventeenth birthday, very immature and naive about the ways of universities in general and black universities in particular."[16]

Graduating in 1955, he worked miscellaneous jobs and assisted his father the following year—all before departing for the Marine Corps in 1956. Reflecting on his four-year stay at Dillard University, Ellis was well aware that music, for a life's work, was viewed by others as a bad decision. When he entered, he was extremely frustrated because he was carrying a lot of baggage.

> I was trying to grow up, relate to girls, adjust to an academic regime, while attempting to learn jazz, which most people considered irrelevant, insignificant, sacriligious and just plain socially unacceptable.[17]

Dillard was a nurturing environment. The students were allowed to grow into young adulthood relatively unscathed by the pressures of racism that existed in the outside world.

A review of Ellis's scrapbook and a glance at his studio walls reveal a great deal: he is an involved person, a giving person, a respected and appreciated person; his opinions are valued and are often solicited. He has been a frequent panelist for the music program of the National Endowment for the Arts and New Orleans Arts Council's Mayoralty Forum—The Arts and City Government and a presenter at the Modern Language Association ("Blues") and the ERIC (Educational Resources Information Centers) session during the Convention of the Conference on College Composition and Communication.

He was a participant in the Jazz Forum of the Congressional Black Caucus (D.C.), New Orleans Very Special Arts Festival—Steering Committee, the March of Dimes National Telethon Against Birth Defects, Teach for America Week, and the New York Philharmonic's 1988 Conference in Harriman, N.Y. ("Toward Greater Participation of Black Americans in Symphony Orchestras"). The Young Leadership Council of New Orleans designated Ellis Marsalis as one of twenty-five "role models" in 1991. The Young Leadership Council is a nonprofit group that fosters leadership skills in young people by tackling community issues.

Special Ellis Marsalis performances have taken place at New Orleans and Louisiana inaugural activities, the NAACP Convention (New Orleans), Studio Museum of Harlem, and Harvard University's "Learning from Performance" Program. The certificate of recognition of his service as visiting artist at Harvard was signed and presented by President Derek Bok. Ellis returned to Richmond, Virginia, in 1994 (five years following his three teaching years at Virginia Commonwealth University) to perform at Innsbrook, benefitting the Virginia Foundation for the Exceptional Child and Adolescent.

Honors have been bestowed on Ellis in the form of honorary degrees—Dillard University and Ball State; music's honor society, Pi Kappa Lambda, south central region (1994 Artist Award); a citation of merit presented by the instrumental music fraternity Mu Phi Epsilon; and the Betty Warner Service Award presented by the United Negro College Fund.

Those who know Ellis are well aware that he is a person with a point of view. They also know that he will not hesitate to make known that point of view. He keeps abreast of local, national, and international events. Good examples of his reactions to local events would be the following "Letters to the Editor" from *The Times-Picayune* (New Orleans):

Support Arts in Schools (September 3, 1992)

As chairman of the Louisiana Music Commission, I see an opportunity for the incoming Orleans Parish School Board to express their philosophy regarding the arts as an integral part of a student's basic education.

New Orleans is touted as the "City of Jazz," yet there is limited support for the serious study of music in pre-college academics. (New Orleans Center for Creative Arts is not sufficient for the 80,000 plus students in the Orleans Parish school system.)

I am sure the same can be said of the other art disciplines (visual arts, dance, creative writing and theatre).

While music is my area of focus, supporting the arts collectively helps everyone. It is true that a rising tide lifts all ships.

Support instruction in the arts in public education!

Ellis L. Marsalis Jr.

Questions Crime Reports (September 15, 1993)

As a native New Orleanian, I am concerned about the consistency of your coverage of African-Americans who run afoul of the law.

Your meticulous printing of photographs, rap sheets, the recent drawing of an attempted escapee have over the years commanded front-page attention. I am as supportive of the people's right to know as anyone else, but I find this type of coverage to be exemplary of paranoia.

Is this front-page news? Are there more important situations and events pertaining to our city more deserving of front-page coverage?

If reporting crime as front-page news is as important as it appears to be, are African-American males the only criminals in New Orleans or just the only criminals worthy of front-page coverage?

Yours is the leading daily newspaper in our city, but this practice has the appearance of irresponsible journalism at a time when we need responsible leadership from every area.

Ellis L. Marsalis Jr.

Passing the Jazz Torch (November 22, 1993)

Thank you for your recent series on jazz.

As a member of many organizations dedicated to the music of this great state, I often encounter those who think our music will be passed on from generation to generation simply because it exists. Well, it's not that simple.

As your articles pointed out, the passing of the torch is taking place in garages, practice rooms and precious few music venues. I'm sure the world thinks we in Louisiana are taking good care of music, since it is our single greatest contribution to the cultures of the world, but we aren't.

It is especially tragic that our schools are not offering music. The recent cuts inflicted on the arts, music and libraries in our school system represent the mistaken notion that these programs are less important than math or science. Nothing could be further from the truth.

If we are serious about improving education in this state so that our citizens can compete in a world economy, we must mandate arts education. Or else there will be fewer and fewer people capable not only of playing our treasured jazz but of calculating the odds on a bet.

Ellis Marsalis Jr.
Chairman
Louisiana Music Commission

• 2 •

Career Highlights

$\mathcal{A}$fter graduating from Dillard University in 1955, Ellis spent the next months "gigging" around the city and working a bit in his father's business. These activities occupied his time until he, drummer Edward Blackwell, and saxophonist Harold Battiste left the Crescent City for Los Angeles. According to Battiste, one of the people the group "hung out with" was saxophonist Ornette Coleman. Battiste points out:

> In Los Angeles, we paid dues, woodshedded, paid more dues, gigged one night a week . . . sometimes, and then paid still more dues. After about three months, Ellis had to return to New Orleans to help operate his father's motel, Marsalis Mansion. The L.A. experience had been a good one for Ellis. Our early experiments with Ornette Coleman's music and playing during that period made the environment intensely creative. It was the germination of what was to become "Free Jazz."[1]

Shortly thereafter, Ellis joined the Marines and gave two years to Uncle Sam and his country. He was sent to California, where he played clarinet. It was soon discovered that he played piano equally well; and when the band lost its pianist, Ellis was called into service. The United States Marine Corps offered Ellis some wonderful experiences. While stationed at El Toro (a Marine air base in Santa Ana, California), he performed weekly with a group of Marine musicians on a television show called "Dress Blues" (KNXT-CBS) and a radio show called "Leatherneck Songbook" (KFI-NBC). These shows originated from Hollywood. Over a two-year period, a few of the featured performers were singer Connie Stevens, trumpeter Gerald Wilson, saxophonist Eric Dolphy, reedman Buddy Collette, saxophonist Paul Horn, drummer Chico Hamilton, and violinist Stuff Smith.

Following his discharge from the military, he returned to New Orleans. The highlight of 1958 was of course his marriage to Dolores Ferdinand, of which more will be said later. He engaged in private piano study with two

11

Dillard University faculty members, Drs. Philip Rice and Ralph Simpson. He also resumed his private teaching—piano, jazz improvisation, and music theory. Most importantly, he resumed playing with the American Jazz Quintet, which included Alvin Batiste on clarinet, Harold Battiste on saxophone, Peter Badie on bass, Edward Blackwell on drums, and, of course, Ellis on piano.

Since Ellis Marsalis is recognized as one of the nation's leading jazz educators, let us first consider his classroom experiences. Teaching has always been important to Ellis. He once stated, "I have to teach. . . . Jazz is mission, not money." The year 1963 found him teaching at the John H. Martin (formerly Shrewsbury) High School in Jefferson Parish. According to Ellis:

> I wanted to start a band, but the principal gave me two science classes and some general music stuff. If I can't help some student, I am definitely not going to cripple anybody. I left at the end of the year.[2]

With his one-year tenure completed at John H. Martin, he sought employment elsewhere. John Fernandez was band director at the George W. Carver High School in Cajun country, Breaux Bridge (Louisiana). Fernandez was leaving for Opelousa (Louisiana). Roger Dickerson (perhaps Ellis's best friend) and Ellis decided to drive to Breaux Bridge and investigate. Ellis was hired, though the superintendent noted that he needed one more unit of strings for certification. And as he recalls, it was interesting that Carver High School did not have a string program then and had no plans for securing one. His assignment was as bandmaster and choral director and it lasted for two years (1964-66).

> I decided to secure the additional string unit by enrolling at the University of Southwestern Louisiana (Lafayette). You needed four units, three of which I already had. These units I secured at Xavier University, studying cello with the composer, arranger and producer William Fisher.[3]

Ellis's cello instructor at the University of Southwestern Louisiana was Mrs. M. LeBlanc, a violinist. Early in the "cello studying" relationship, Mrs. LeBlanc suggested that Ellis participate in the USL orchestra; they were short of cellos. "If I recall correctly, it was a fairly good university orchestra. The director was Dr. James Burke."[4]

Ellis and his family returned to New Orleans in 1966, by which time the family had grown to include two additional sons—Ellis III and Delfeayo. The next significant teaching experience was at the New Orleans Center for Creative Arts (NOCCA), beginning in the fall of 1974 and continuing through academic year 1985–1986. Since NOCCA has become a model for similar programs throughout the country, more should be said about it. A thorough discussion appears in Al Kennedy's dissertation (1996) at the University of New Orleans. Titled *Jazz Mentors: Public School Teachers and the Musical Tradition of New Orleans*, Chapter 4, "Urban Institutions and Cultural Creativity: Jazz and the Early Development of the New Orleans Center for the Creative Arts," covers well both NOCCA and our subject, Ellis Marsalis, who served on Kennedy's dissertation committee.[5]

NOCCA officially opened January 28, 1974, becoming the first publicly funded school in New Orleans to offer jazz as an integral part of the curriculum. Funding came from the National Endowment for the Arts and the Louisiana Music Therapy Fund. The musicians' union made it possible to bring musicians into classrooms at thirty-one public schools. Clarinetist Alvin Batiste was the first jazz-artist-in-residence in the United States. NOCCA provided professional training in dance, music, theater, visual arts, and creative writing. According to the 1979–1980 edition of its *Student Guide*, its goals were:

1. In-depth training in dance, music, theater, visual arts, or writing, which includes instilling in each student a high degree of self-sufficiency.
2. Knowledge of artistic skills, enabling students to make judgments about vocations and avocations in the arts.
3. Some understanding of the nature of all of the arts.

In August 1974, Ellis was contacted by clarinetist Alvin Batiste and informed about a job—with NOCCA—in which he might be interested. His initial reaction was "not very enthusiastic."

> I had spent the first summer session at Loyola University, pursuing a master's degree. The chairman of Xavier's music department promised me a full time position if I earned a master's degree. I had been a lecturer at Xavier University, developing a course in Afro-American music. Actually it was really a jazz course which did not include sacred music or the more formally composed music from the African American tradition.[6]

The GI Bill made it possible for him to return to the classroom, all expenses paid. "I had never used my school opportunities from a financial standpoint." Ellis and his wife Dolores had discussed the pursuit of another degree and were not ready to give up on the idea. It was Dolores who felt he should go for the NOCCA interview. "I earned a total of nine hours that summer (1974), and I had a plan for the first time that did not center around hustling gigs," something that was very gratifying.

At NOCCA, Ellis's duties were to provide music students with lessons in learning jazz skills. He soon realized that his formal education did not prepare him for developing lesson plans for jazz study, despite his student teaching experience. He also realized that the students exiting high school in the 1970s were not passionate about jazz. Reflecting on the NOCCA experience, Ellis indicated:

> NOCCA was a completely new experience for me. The old adage "be careful what you wish for because you just might get it" was a perfect description for my introduction to an arts magnet high school. Since the high school musicians during my school days were discouraged from playing jazz, I mistakenly thought that having a program that formally introduced jazz techniques would be cause for celebration. I assumed these students would eagerly embrace the music of Monk, Miles, Dizzy and Bird. I was in for a rude awakening.

Ellis pointed out that, in time, he came to understand several things:

1. The pop music of the day was performed primarily on electronic instruments, which were constantly being modified to meet the demands of the young players searching for hit recordings.
2. The role of acoustic instruments was reduced to a secondary one to the extent that the primary sound of pop music was electrified.
3. Live music venues either eliminated or did not purchase pianofortes, choosing to hire only groups that were self-contained.
4. Inadequate pay scales in public education had caused a decline in the more talented music instructors. There was also a low expectation of music excellence. The marching band became the primary reference of excellence.[7]

It was necessary that Ellis develop a curriculum for NOCCA. The approach was totally random. To his knowledge, there were no books on teaching jazz in high school. "We were never certain of our available instrumentation, since students were accepted by audition."

NOCCA was established by a federal grant, secured by Shirley Trusty (Corey). Home base was initially (January 1974) on the campus of the

University of New Orleans. Ellis joined the faculty in the fall of 1974, having missed the first semester. By this time, the program had been moved to a building that was formerly an elementary school in an upscale residential area near St. Charles Avenue, within walking distance of Tulane and Loyola Universities.

A student accepted at NOCCA attends another school for his or her core curriculum. The program consumes three years of the students' high school experience—sophomore, junior, senior. The core curriculum school has to consent to cooperate in terms of scheduling. In terms of the Marsalis boys, Branford attended NOCCA for one and a half years, Wynton for three years, Delfeayo for four years, and Jason for two years.

This is the school that nurtured the talents of Moses Hogan (pianist, composer, and choral director), Rachel Jordan (violinist/Louisiana Philharmonic), Kent Jordan (flutist, recording artist), Harry Connick Jr. (pianist, vocalist, recording artist), Jean Michelle Charbonnet (soprano/Metropolitan Opera), Chris Severin (bassist with Dianne Reeves), Marlon Jordan (trumpeter, recording artist), Terence Blanchard (trumpeter, recording artist, film composer), and Donald Harrison (saxophonist, recording artist).

Activities of the 1960s were particularly significant: From 1961 to 1962 and in 1966, after two years in Breaux Bridge, Ellis returned to New Orleans and worked with Bob Prado (bass) and Joe Morton (drums and vibes), and performed at the PlayBoy Club (New Orleans) with Marshall Smith (bass), Nathaniel Perrilliat (tenor saxophone), and James Black (drums). Ellis was with the Al Hirt Band from 1967–1970, cutting several albums with him and appearing in the movie *Number One*. It is often written that Al Hirt gave Ellis's son Wynton his first trumpet at age six, though he was age twelve before he took the instrument seriously.

Ellis Jr. made several solo appearances with the New Orleans Symphony Orchestra, playing his own composition "Ballad for Jazz Trio and Symphony Orchestra," and works of Duke Ellington. In 1996, Ellis and other performers/composers appeared with the Louisiana Philharmonic Orchestra (formerly New Orleans Symphony). Ellis's works were "Ellington Suite" and "Ballad for Jazz Quartet." In the same year, he performed his "Ballad" with the Chicago Sinfonietta.

To be sure, teaching is not limited to the classroom. Lectures/performances have been and continue to be important in Ellis's schedule. A quick review of his resume shows numerous related activities: Afro-American

Music Lecture at Xavier University 1967–1974, Lecture-Demonstration on Modern Jazz as Compared to Rock and Roll at Tulane University (1966), "Contemporary Jazz Developments" Symposium (1970), Jazz Improvisation Workshop at the Free Southern Theater (1971), Three-day Jazz Improvisation Workshop at Jackson State University (Mississippi, 1972), and National Catholic Convention (1973).

The year 1974 saw lecture/performances at Dominican College and three public high schools (Gateway II, Eleanor McMain, and J. S. Clark). Worth noting are activities between 1982 and 1985: Performance/workshop at Jackson State University with Kenny Burrell (guitar), Dick Griffin (trombone), Nathan Davis (tenor saxophone), Freddie Waits (drums), and others; workshops for the Professional Improvement Program sponsored by the Orleans Parish School Board. There were workshops at Florida State University (Tallahassee) and Northeast Illinois University (Evanston); a workshop with trumpeter Woody Shaw, at Tulane University, Louisiana State University, and Duke University; a three-day residency at the University of Massachusetts at Amherst; and a summer workshop at Indiana University in Pennsylvania. Ellis performed for the Music Educators National Conference (MENC) Convention in Mobile, Alabama, demonstrating techniques and concepts. Performances at the New Orleans Jazz and Heritage Festival have been constant—solo and with established artists, including members of his family.

As word began to spread about Ellis's teaching skills and performance excitement, invitations increased. Most invitations were fulfilled; his activities included a ten-day Summer Arts Program for high school students at Northlake Arts Camp (Ponchatula, La.); the New York City Public Theater with Alvin Batiste (clarinet), Ed Blackwell (drums), Mark Helias (bass), Branford and Wynton Marsalis; the Showcase Lounge (Chicago); Newport Jazz Festival in New York at Waterloo Village; a solo spot at Carnegie Recital Hall; and an appearance at Fort Worth, Texas's, Caravan of Dreams. He performed with the Wynton Marsalis Quintet at Blues Alley (D.C.), as well as Governors State University in Chicago. The Caribbean Jazz Festival in Barbados featured Ellis, Victor Goines (saxophone), Noel Kendrick (drums), and Reginald Veal (bass).

Patriarch Ellis Marsalis Jr. was piano soloist for the first evening of the National Association for the Advancement of Colored People's (NAACP) 1983 Convention, held in New Orleans. As cochairperson of the Music Committee, I guaranteed that all music performed would be by a black composer, with emphasis on New Orleans composers. The "top-notch" pianist complied and offered John Work's "Scuppernong." This was a shock to those who were not aware that Ellis's performances are not limited to any one genre, though his specialty is jazz.

R. Nathaniel Dett (1882–1943) is revered as one of Afro-America's most outstanding "classical" composers. "Dance" (Juba), from his "In the Bottoms" suite, is now "a semi-standard" in piano repertoire. *The Collected Piano Works of R. Nathaniel Dett* was Vivian Flagg McBrier's 1973 published dissertation for Catholic University. The 1996 edition provides us with "Introductions" by Dominique-Rene de Lerma and Vivian Flagg McBrier, as well as a "Foreword" by Ellis Marsalis. The conceivers of this idea were quite wise in their selection, as Ellis broadens the performer's awarenesses and offers an approach not often considered valid. Wrote Ellis, "This music is not 'Classical' in the Eurocentric sense of the word. . . .This collection give[s] us a glimpse of America from Dett's perspective . . . ," with the Negro Spirituals representing, in Dett's words, 'the best class of Negro music.' "[9]

Following the 1987 passing of Concurrent Resolution 57 designating jazz "a rare and valuable American treasure," Congress asked the National Park Service "to conduct a feasibility study to determine ways of preserving and interpreting the origin and history of jazz in New Orleans." Planning for the New Orleans Jazz National Historical Park began in late 1995.

The seventeen-member commission began meeting in January 1996. Recommendations for the commission came from the mayor, recognized experts in music education programs, local businesses associated with tourism, the board of the New Orleans Jazz and Heritage Foundation, and a representative experienced in historic preservation within the city. Also recommended: Two members—one recommended by the Smithsonian Institution and the other by the Louisiana State Museum; two members from local neighborhood groups and local associations; one member representing local mutual aid and benevolent societies and pleasure clubs; one member of the Louisiana State Music Commission; a representative of the New Orleans Jazz Club representing the governor; a recognized local expert on the history, development, and progression of jazz; and as an ex officio member, the commission's superintendent of the Jazz National Historical Park. In addition, two members were recommended by the Smithsonian Institution and the National Endowment for the Arts. Recommended by the Arts Endowment chairman was Ellis Marsalis.

· 3 ·

All in the Family

"The loins of Ellis Marsalis certainly deserve a tip of the hat when it comes to producing jazz-musician progeny, . . ." so reads the lead sentence in a "Limelight" article that appeared in the *Washington Post* on June 20, 1993.[1] Branford, Wynton, Delfeayo, and Jason (plus two nonmusicians, Ellis III and Mboya) were all fathered by Ellis Marsalis and mothered by Dolores Ferdinand Marsalis.

"This Functional Family" is the title of a feature article in *ASCAP Playback*, Summer Issue, 1996. Authors Erik Philbrook and Jim Steinblatt captured well the Marsalis spirit. The question is: What is the Marsalis spirit? On stage, in the studio, they are just plain people, minus celebrity status. It is universally accepted that "Ellis and Dolores Marsalis created a home environment for their children, in which each child was able to discover his niche and thrive."[2] Independence in action and spirit was the byword. The intent of this chapter is to bring truth to these statements by considering the six children independently, and most importantly, their mother, Dolores.

My plan was to have each of the five sons (minus Mboya) put their comments on tape concerning their father, family experiences, growing up in the Marsalis household, one-on-one interactions with their father, adult relationships, and their assessment of their father's place in history. The following letter was sent to each of the five children:

August 15, 1996

I am in the process of completing a biography of your father, Ellis Marsalis Jr. To date, he and I have completed three (3) one-hour sessions, the last being this past Monday (8/12/96). It was at that time that I secured your address and telephone number, as well as assurance from him that he would prepare each of you for this correspondence. Since you are busy and in the interest of time, I thought it conceivable for you to talk into a tape recorder.

19

Please return the tape to me at your earliest convenience. I will take your ideas from the tape. Should there be questions, I will make contact via telephone. I am interested in any and everything that you would like to share about 1) growing up in the Marsalis household; 2) your father's influence on you personally (his philosophies on life, etc.); 3) with the exception of Ellis III and Mboya, your father's influence on you musically; and 4) your assessment of his place in history.

I have known your father for many years. I am a native New Orleanian, a strong admirer of Ellis Jr., and former director of the National Endowment for the Arts' Music Program. Your father can share with you more on the subject. Please know that I have assured him that nothing will be sent to the publisher without his consent. One chapter will be devoted to Ellis and Dolores's sons, and Dolores.

encl. blank tape

Signed: D. Antoinette Handy

Such was my plan, but it did not work. The next effort was to hold telephone conversations. Here I met with limited success. There were direct telephone contacts with Wynton, Ellis III, and Delfeayo. Additionally, brief discussions were held with Jason, but never on this specific topic. Dr. David Swanzy of the Loyola University music faculty was successful in getting an interview with Jason, which was devoted exclusively to his father. With a wealth of newspaper and magazine clippings, I felt that I had sufficient information and could produce a meaningful biography. I also knew that Ellis Jr. had fantastic recall abilities and wrote well. He willingly assisted and was available whenever I sought his attention. Since music is the primary engagement of four of his sons, it should be emphasized that Ellis never urged his sons to become musicians, but made certain that they were exposed to good music and the best of teachers.

BRANFORD

Born August 26, 1960, Branford Iweanya Marsalis was at a young age attracted to reed instruments. Initially, he studied the piano with none other than Ellis Jr., his father. He switched to clarinet and then to saxophone. Branford has since distinguished himself as a gifted saxophonist (primarily tenor and soprano), talented leader, composer, and film actor. Ellis Jr. has confessed that Branford has many of his early musical traits, whereas Wynton's discipline draws on the determination of Dolores, his wife. On at least

Ellis's father, Ellis Sr.

Ellis's mother, Florence Marie Robertson Marsalis.

A bit on the chubby side, baby Ellis.

Ellis decked out in his Gilbert Academy uniform, 1948.

Yvette Marsalis and big brother Ellis.

Ellis, cheerful and charming.

Teenaged Marsalis and younger sister Yvette.

Ellis in young manhood.

"Messing around" (Ellis isn't certain, but believes this piano belonged to one of his teachers).

From clarinet to tenor saxophone.

Xavier Junior School of Music's orchestra, 1946, Ellis on clarinet (circled). Photo courtesy of Al Kennedy, photo by Bedov.

Branford, held by his maternal grandmother.

*Parents Ellis and Dolores, with sons
Wynton and Branford at Disneyland.*

Mr. Songemas from the Congo and a state department representative dine at the Marsalis Motel. Young Ellis tries to follow the conversation.

MARSALIS' MANSION

The Motel of Distinction

110 SHREWSBURY ROAD   **VE 5-3161**

- WALL-TO-WALL CARPETING
- AIR CONDITIONING
- TELEPHONE IN ROOMS

- FREE TV
- FREE PARKING
- TILE BATH AND SHOWER

We are overlooking the mighty Mississippi River
Just 10 minutes from downtown New Orleans
Just outside of the hustle and bustle of city noises
Come and spend a quiet weekend at "The Mansion" in gala old New Orleans

★

Filet Mignon

Sirloin Steaks

Minute Steaks

Sea Foods

★

THE RIVER ROOM OF MARSALIS' MANSION

★

Exquisite Martinis

Imported Beer

Scotch Hi-Balls

Brandy Cocktails

★

- NEW ORLEANS' MOST EXQUISITE STEAK HOUSE
- DINE IN A LAVISH ATMOSPHERE OF ROYALTY
- WE HONOR AMERICAN EXPRESS CREDIT CARDS

Advertisement for Marsalis' Mansion.

Ellis (third from left, next to Hirt) with Al Hirt's band, on the lawn of the White House, following an appearance inside.

Ellis on the road with Al Hirt's band, idling the time away in Ellicott City, Md.

Ellis and Sonny Stitt, with Wynton and Branford Marsalis, attending the New Orleans Jazz and Heritage Festival.

Wynton, Noel Dolliole, Ellis, and Branford at NOCCA, 1978.

Ellis's early performing years.

Original Storyville Jazz Band (Ellis is standing on the far right).

Ellis performing at the Hyatt Regency in New Orleans between 1978 and 1980.

one occasion, Branford said of himself, "I'm really lazy. I'm not talking about lazy in terms of not working. I'm talking about not studying, not looking into things. That's what I mean by lazy."[3]

During the course of the same interview, Branford discussed the word "jazz," and how he fit into that picture:

> I never really felt like I had to say "I'm a jazz musician," because I always listened to all different kinds of music and I've always played in all kinds of musical situations. I think that jazz music is the hardest kind of music I've ever tried to play and it's my first love because of that . . . jazz musicians don't run around clamoring to call themselves something they are not . . . so many people try to grab on to the name jazz. Because they love the sound of it but they don't really want to play it and they don't really want to pay the dues for it and I think that's where the big rift comes in . . . I know what jazz is and I also know what it is not and I love to hear it played right.[4]

Following high school, he attended Southern University in Baton Rouge (La.) for one year. His roommate was New Orleans saxophonist Donald Harrison and his instructor, acclaimed clarinetist Alvin Batiste. He then matriculated at Berklee College of Music in Boston (1979–1980). Branford performed with Art Blakey's big band during the summer of 1980, playing the baritone saxophone. He spent time with Lionel Hampton and did gigs with Clark Terry, Dizzy Gillespie, and Miles Davis. For about six months, he was a member of Blakey's Jazz Messengers (along with brother Wynton) and was a member of brother Wynton's quintet for approximately three years.

He was a founding member of the English rock singer/electric guitarist Sting's band. His three and a half years with Sting culminated with his *Tonight Show* adventure. Many believe that the Sting experience better prepared him for his next association. Branford signed a five-year contract with the *Tonight Show* (NBC) and its host Jay Leno in 1992.

Saxophonist Branford replaced trumpeter Doc Severinsen as the show's music director. Chances were good that Branford Marsalis would become a household name, with audiences of eight to ten million nightly. He terminated his contract just over the midway point. According to the press, he did not wish to continue as Leno's sidekick, and his nine-year-old son wanted to return to the East Coast.

Branford then formed his own quartet, which met with much success. He made his film debut in Spike Lee's *She's Gotta Have It*, followed by *School Daze*. Another acting success was in Danny DeVito's *Throw Mama from the Train*.

Branford has performed with various orchestras, including the Boston Pops and the English Chamber Orchestra. In 1996, both father and son recorded the CD "Loved Ones," in which they expressed the view that no generation gap exists between them, musically or emotionally. At Borders Bookstore in Los Angeles, shortly following the CD's release, the two explained that "Loved Ones" is devoted to "the romantic effect of ladies upon American songwriters."

Branford had this to say about the experience:

> It's great to be in a situation where I can be around my father and confront him as a man, not as a boy. . . . Working on this music together, he's had to confront my ideas about music, and a lot of what we do with the songs is based on my ideas. . . . Of course . . . he never lets me forget something he always used to say when we were kids. "Son," he told us, "the thing you are going to have to learn is that life has a foot for every butt."[5]

Branford says of his father:

> [He] is a stickler for history. He insists that it is through the past that one learns the future. By studying the history of the music, you can better develop your abilities in whatever field with fewest mistakes.[6]

He also states:

> My dad, like a lot of Americans, was raised to get "a craft." You find one thing to do, and you do that. My father's point to me has always been this: the amount of time that I have spent working on other things shows a certain level of extraordinary ability, but that ability would best be suited in the jazz world, because there is an absolute paucity of quality jazz musicians.[7]

On another occasion, his father prepared him for certain realities related to racism:

> My father told me about race and society at an early age. When all these white kids in my high school were screwing up, he took me aside and said, "Look, your friend, his father owns a car dealership. If he screws up, he still has a job. I'm a school teacher, son. You screw up, when you come out, you have nothing. It's your choice."[8]

One recent performance was broadcast by National Public Radio and WBGO in Newark, supported by the Lila Wallace–Reader's Digest Fund with additional support from the National Endowment for the Arts, Columbia Jazz, and Verve Records. The ad announcing it read, " Extraordinary Host;

Exceptional Music; Exclusively on Jazzset." Most recently (during the fall semester, 1998–1999), Branford would instruct and coach students at Michigan State University. He continues to grow and engage in new experiences.

When I was unable to make direct contact with Branford, younger brother Delfeayo shared with me Branford's recall of a football experience where his father played an important role:

> In spite of *The Bell Curve*, I don't really believe that white people think that we are as inferior as they say we are. If they really felt that we were inferior, they would open the floodgates and give us equal access.
>
> When we played for the Lions Club at Morgan Park, we didn't have a park and they did. All of our uniforms were hand-me-downs from them. They felt Christian because they were passing down their old uniforms. We did not have the ways or means to procure facilities, equipment, training and coaching that was adequate enough to compete on a real level. They had a full time coach, a defensive coordinator, and a complete staff. We had one n----- who they paid $25 a game. He sat on his car and drank beer. He allowed Daddy to come on the field and diagram the plays.
>
> Daddy came 'cause the coach didn't show up and the referee said you gotta have a coach or it's a forfeit. Daddy said "I'll coach." We had the only car, so daddy had to make several trips to go get kids—drop kids off, go get kids, drop kids off. We start the game and daddy goes in the huddle. Daddy asks, "Who's the center?" No one raises their hand. "Who shifts the ball?" The cat says to me, "All right, you are the center? Who stands next to the center? You are a guard. Who stands next to him? You are the tackle."
>
> Now all of a sudden there is an intellectual cohesiveness that's occurring at the spur of the moment. They scored the first touchdown, 7–0. Then we scored a touchdown, but missed the extra point. They were about to punt the ball, when Daddy says "You know, I'm backed up to do the punt thing." He said, "Do an end-around. Whoever catches the ball, run to the opposite side and pass the ball to the other guy." Then there were two minutes left in the game and we were on the 6 yard line, 5 yard line, and we ran one play when the ref blew the whistle. We felt that a moral victory had occurred. They had everything; we had nothing. There was just Daddy having the wherewithal intellectually to put us in the same philosophical ballpark with them. It changed everything about the game—affirmative action at work.[9]

WYNTON

Wynton Learson Marsalis, trumpeter, composer, conductor, recording artists, educator, and second child of Ellis and Dolores Marsalis, was born October 18, 1961. He rose to the forefront of instrumental acclaim in the early 1980s. In June 1996, *Time* magazine listed Wynton as one of "America's 25 Most Influential People." The following month, *Life* magazine listed Wynton as one of "The 50 Most Influential Boomers." The opening sentence of "Notes on Wynton Marsalis" for the 1996 Olympic Arts Festival read, "Wynton Marsalis has by force of personality, intelligence and achievement brought jazz back to center stage in America."[10]

Wynton appeared on the cover of *Time* magazine, October 22, 1990. The accompanying article emphasized:

> But the most significant thing about Marsalis's career is not his personal success. It is the fact that, largely under his influence, a jazz renaissance is flowering on what was once barren soil. Straight-ahead jazz music almost died in the 1970s. . . . Now a whole generation of prodigiously talented young musicians is going back to the roots, using acoustic instruments, playing recognizable tunes, and studying the styles of earlier jazzmen.[11]

Dan Morgenstern, director of the Institute of Jazz Studies at Rutgers University, reminds us that, "Young men can now make a living playing straight-ahead jazz, and Wynton is responsible for that being possible." George Butler, then Columbia Records executive producer, stated that, "Wynton has played a major role in the popularity of this music today. This is probably the most propitious time for this music since the '50s and early '60s." Pianist, composer, and jazz commentator Billy Taylor stated, "Wynton is the most important young spokesman for the music today. His opinions are well founded."[12]

Wynton is currently artistic director of jazz at Lincoln Center in New York City and leader of the Lincoln Center Jazz Orchestra. He was also named the first minister of culture for the city of New Orleans by the mayor in 1996. Early in 1998, it was formally announced that "New York [City] Plans to Build a Concert Hall for Jazz, the First of its Kind," in keeping with jazz's designation as "a rare and valuable national American treasure."

After wandering in the desert of Lincoln Center for seven years:

> the organization's youngest constituent, Jazz at Lincoln Center, seems closer to finding a home of its own. Mayor Rudolph W. Giuliani announced at a news conference . . . that projected new development plans for the New York Coliseum site at Columbus Circle would house a 100,000 square foot space for the seven-year-old program, whose artistic director is the trumpeter Wynton Marsalis.[13]

Wynton must be credited with having brought dignity to the art form by heightening jazz awareness throughout the world. As he states, "Jazz is a way of life that continually challenges you to strive for perfection and illumination, even after the music stops."[14] The Lincoln Center Jazz Orchestra tours throughout the country and across Europe and Asia.

The Wynton Marsalis work that the orchestra toured between January and March 1997 was "Blood on the Fields," an epic oratorio based on American slavery, commissioned by Lincoln Center. This is the work that won for Wynton a Pulitzer prize in April 1997, which represented a first for jazz.

His early training and experience began with participation in the Fairview Baptist Church Band led by guitarist Danny Barker. Given his first trumpet at age six (by the famed trumpeter Al Hirt), he did not become serious about music until age twelve. Two years later, he performed the Haydn Trumpet Concerto with the New Orleans Symphony and, two years after that, the Brandenburg Concerto No. 2 with the same orchestra. Wynton acquired significant experience in various marching, jazz, and funk bands, as well as classical youth orchestras.

At age fifteen, he attended Eastern Music Festival in North Carolina, where he earned the "Most Outstanding Musician Award." Following high school graduation, he attended Tanglewood in Massachusetts. He then entered Juilliard (1979), during which time he played with the Brooklyn Philharmonic and the pit band of "Sweeney Todd." Around this time, he soloed with the Mexico City Symphony.[15]

As with his father, education is a priority. Extremely popular is his sold-out Saturday morning "Jazz for Young People" series at Lincoln Center. He has conducted master classes throughout the country. Well received were his four music-appreciation programs (1995), filmed and conceived by him. He wrote a companion book to the PBS series entitled "Marsalis on Music" for W. W. Norton. Also well received was the National Public Radio twenty-six-part series entitled "Making the Music."

He chronicled his touring life in the 1994 book *Sweet Swing Blues: On the Road*. Along the way, he discusses some members of his family. Regarding Branford, he recalled growing up together in Kenner, Louisiana, playing clarinet and trumpet.

> In high school we played together in a funk band, the Creators. We played many, many dances, weddings, proms, battles of the bands, and talent shows, and had a thoroughly good time socially. We loved playing together . . .
>
> But even more than playing together, we grew up together a certain way. Our personalities developed to fit each other. I was hot and fiery, ready to curse somebody out . . . Book (Branford's nickname) was cool and diplomatic: "Man, if you just shut your mouth, we'll be cool." . . . We slept in the same room until Branford went off to college. That was the loneliest year of my life.[16]

The word "mama" takes on special meaning, personally and universally.

> Mother and child discovering the world again and for the first time. This has a special glow. . . . She is your safety net. Even in failure, you are still loved. . . . A good, hot, home-cooked supper represents more than just basic survival. Even when you argue at the table, it is romantic, prepared with love and style. They say that the greatest chefs are men. But we know that the best meals are to be had in the many homes presided over by her who has the greatest stake in our development. This is the end of the twentieth century. You will hear that men and women are the same. It is not yet true.[17]

Wynton shares with his readers the following concerning his brother Mboya. At morning time in New Orleans:

> Mboya keeps his eye on Mr. Ellis [the father]. Mboya is autistic. He never talks, only sighs through his nose like a miniature steam engine. He jumps up and organizes anything out of place in a room . . . You almost never know what he is thinking, except in this instance his thoughts will soon become ours.[18]

Taking a leave of absence from the Juilliard School in 1979, Wynton joined Art Blakey and the Jazz Messengers. Wynton did a six-week festival and a concert tour with the Herbie Hancock Quartet. He secured his first record contract from Columbia in 1981. To date, he has been the recipient of eight Grammy Awards, eight honorary doctorate degrees, France's Grand Prix du Disque, the Netherlands' Edison Award, and the Paul Hume (music critic, the *Washington Post*) Award. In 1995, Wynton performed before the United Nations Press Club and was the first artist to be awarded Grammys in both the classical and jazz categories. Wynton has appeared with many of the world's great orchestras, including Philadelphia, Cleveland, Los Angeles, San Francisco, New York Philharmonic, St. Louis, and Detroit Symphony Orchestras.

For his tenth recording release, "Standard Time Volume Three—The Resolution of Romance," Wynton teamed up with his father and shared this information with a local journalist:

> I always wanted to do an album with my father because I grew up listening to his sound, and I have a lot of respect for him as a musician, . . . I was just waiting to develop enough sophistication to handle those songs well enough to play with him.[19]

To date, he has recorded more than thirty jazz and classical albums for Columbia and Sony Classical. His jazz groups have appeared in thirty countries, on six continents. His film credits include, as composer, *Tune in To-morrow*, *The Wright Brothers at Kitty Hawk*, and *Shannon's Deal* (NBC–TV). In conjunction with Lincoln Center Chamber Music Society, he composed "Jazz: Six Syncopated Movements" for the New York City Ballet. He recently composed his first string quartet, "At the Octoroon Balls," for the Orion String Quartet, in conjunction with the Lincoln Center Chamber Music Society.

During a telephone conversation on September 17, 1996, Wynton had this to offer:

> I grew up going to gigs with my father—at Al Hirt's Place, Lu and Charlie's, Crazy Shirley's, and other such places. There were never a lot of people, but it really didn't matter to my father. In some respects, I hated going to these places mainly because I didn't like that kind of music. But I enjoyed being the only young one—hanging out with the musicians.

I inquired about his opinion of his father's style—changes and consistencies:

> He has been consistent, yet there have been some changes (for the better). He has matured; he is more relaxed. . . . These were rough times in the Marsalis household, with all these children and an autistic child. . . . On the subject of education, so much of what I do is based on what he [my father] did. [20]

I inquired about the father's means of communicating with the children. Said Wynton, "He talked to us as if we were men, never condescending."

Because of Wynton's professorial approach to things, I was curious about his early education. "I attended St. Joan of Arc for nursery school; first and second grades were at Martinez; third through seventh, Our Lady of Perpetual Help; eighth and ninth, De LaSalle; tenth, eleventh and twelfth, Benjamin Franklin High School." The last three years were also spent at the New Orleans Center for Creative Arts (NOCCA).

> I didn't take any classes with him except ensemble and ear training. My father has a real relaxed way of teaching. When he would stop talking, the students would start playing funk. Students didn't want to learn.

I inquired about some of the students who were in attendance when he was at NOCCA and his reaction to his father's three-year stay in Richmond, Virginia:

> Flutist Kent Jordan was there before my group. Those who were there during my time included Jonathan Bloom, Miles Wright, Donald Harrison and

Terence Blanchard. My father's plans to go to Virginia were somewhat strange. Initially, I was shocked. Ellis Marsalis has a lot of integrity. He is the least pretentious person that I know. He believes in the music. His involvement is not for accolades or money. He is a frustrated intellectual. He sticks with what he believes. Our home was filled with problems. It was rough on everybody. The media writes about "the first family of jazz" and all that b.s. This type of thing can put a lot of pressure on you.[21]

In closing, I expressed my sincere thanks and indicated that I thought he would be the hardest to get a hold of. Wynton inquired "Why?" and I answered "Too busy." His response: "For my dad?"

ELLIS III

The third son is Ellis Louis Marsalis III, born August 18, 1964. We met in Washington, D.C., when he served as a lay panelist on a National Endowment for the Arts music panel. I recall being extremely impressed with his charming personality. Something special was laid on him as it was on the other sons. The Ellis and Dolores touch was evident. Also, I was impressed with his knowledge of the subject at hand—jazz—though he is not a practicing musician.

If there was a connection between a panelist and an applicant at the National Endowment for the Arts, the law then required that the panelist had to step out of the room during the deliberations, scoring, and funding recommendations. Consequently, Ellis III was out of the room most of the time, since "a Marsalis" name appeared in so many applications in that category (jazz). He remarked, "Well it's good to see that my father and brothers are working." The procedure now requires that a person not serve on the panel if such conflicts seem apparent when putting a panel together.

Ellis III is a computer consultant and is president of Network Engineer/Polaris Systems in Baltimore, Maryland. He has been interested in computers since high school, mainly because of their complexities.

When preparing this publication, I decided to ask Ellis III to simply talk about himself and his father, while I recorded our conversation. Following is a summary of his statements (Baltimore, Maryland, and Jackson, Mississippi), September 1, 1996:

I attended Catholic schools (elementary and secondary) and played the guitar and flute in music classes. The ole man didn't encourage any of us to go into music. His theory was, "Think about what you want to do." It never occurred to me to pursue a career in music. "One doesn't pick music; music picks them."

What I remember most about my father is that he was very big and had a commanding presence. He talked to the boys in a group, about any and everything. I can't remember the topics, but they made sense later on. It was not so much what he was saying as the fact that he was saying something. Mother was around but was not in on the conversations. She might come in to say, "Let them go to bed," but she had no other involvement.

Upon high school graduation, I joined the military and later worked for the police department as a paramedic. I had extensive ROTC involvement. Then, I moved to New York City to enroll at New York University. Originally I majored in English and history. But the English didn't pan out.

There was very little "American" literature (perhaps 3 out of 10 courses offered). I stuck, however, with the history, graduating in 1988. I then put in more military time, but again, in the Reserves.

Generally, I'm the last one that people meet. They say, "So you're Ellis III. I've met your brothers and even some of your cousins, but never you." I'm always glad it happens, in a bizarre kind of way. I've never wanted to be a part of the musical scene. I remember one time an interviewer wanted to talk with each of us, since they were doing a piece on the family. But I soon realized that it was not really about the family, merely an angle they could get for their story. I was headed for work. They asked me if I wanted to participate. Obviously it really didn't matter if I did or did not. I said "No, not really." My mother was furious. Remember, it was a family story.[22]

It was during this telephone conversation that Ellis III expressed his disgust over the "cashing in" idea. (See the preface.)

DELFEAYO

I met son Delfeayo when he was in his mid-teens. His father was having him observe a Saturday morning band program, one in which my son was participating. For Delfeayo, there was no participation, only observation. Born July 28, 1965, Delfeayo Ferdinand Marsalis has distinguished himself as a trombonist and a jazz record producer. The *Washington Post* referred to Delfeayo as "a jack-of-all-trades"—composer, producer, trombone player, and in mid-1993, host of a cable TV series.[23]

As early as age seventeen, he produced his father's record "Syndrome." Since then, he has produced records for Harry Connick, Marcus Roberts, Kenny Kirkland, Terence Blanchard, Donald Harrison, and Branford and

Ellis Marsalis to name a few. He was also associate producer of Spike Lee's movies *Do the Right Thing* and *A Love Supreme*. Delfeayo is today one of the most prominent acoustic jazz producers in the business.

He graduated from Boston's Berklee College of Music. Filled with self-determination and dedication, he reminds us that these are Marsalis traits. "My father always told us one thing: 'If you can't be the best, don't do it.'"[24] Delfeayo often leads his own ensemble.

Telephone contact was finally made in early February 1998. He agreed to provide me with material from which I could extract what was usable. Under the heading "Negroid Fatherhood" he wrote:

> The summer when I was eight years old and my brother Ellis, nine, was indeed an adventurous one. At some point during those three long months, my parents took us into the country for a rather extended visit with some of our lesser-known relatives. As we drove through Mississippi one scorching hot day, we happened upon a voluptuous and inviting cotton field. My father, in all of his wisdom, stopped the car by the roadside, then offered, "Why don't y'all go ahead and pick some cotton?" . . . The cotton is hidden by leaves, which are protected by thorns—plenty of thorns, both large and small. We walked back to the car, dismayed and disgusted, confused and concerned that our father could subject us to such treachery. . . . As we finally made it back to our broken down and faded Chevrolet, my mother greeted us with kisses and a few crumpled up tissues, wiping Ellis's hands and comforting my tears. Of course, old dad let us internalize the situation before stating in his nonchalant tone, "Whenever you think about bullshitting . . . remember that."
>
> I would come to realize that my father, Ellis Jr., raised his six sons in accordance with one basic principle: He doesn't know everything, but he knows more than me or you. Such is the case with any elder. Rather than concentrate on the activities of other folks, Ellis has a way of making *you* feel responsible. "Daddy, I sure wish somebody would do something about. . . ." "Son, did it ever occur to you that if you don't do it, no one else will?" Of course, Ellis's questions are not asked to be answered.
>
> While he is often prone to share his vast knowledge of politics and life, those examples which most accurately define his philosophical views are always concise and unadorned. Yes, Ellis is a man of both many words and few words, a believer in a sharp pencil, an old dictionary, and a big stick. In the tradition of great Negro preachers, he is able to present a coherent story, dip into related and unrelated issues, tie up the loose ends and rake you home with a shout chorus.
>
> I have provided commentary with virtually no reference to my mother Dolores. That's primarily because Dolores deserves her own chapter or

maybe even a complete book. Emotional Dolores and provocative Ellis . . . . Yes, what a perfect couple Mom and Dad make. . . . Mild mannered Ellis and uncompromising Dolores.

Although I look to old Dad for guidance in every conceivable capacity, he is quite a difficult man to describe. Man first, father second, musician third. I would venture to say that the most successful aspect of his parenting was not burdening six sons with the personal judgment and character defamation that often accompanies parental supervision. Rather than incessant nagging, Ellis showed by example. . . . Believe me, Ellis wore the pants in the house, yet was always supportive of his sons' decisions, whether he agreed with them or not.

My father, like his father, is a very proud man. In his catalogue of stories, the ones pertaining to segregation are not always the most frequent, but amongst my favorites. Ellis will tell you about riding behind the "colored only" screens with a hint of melancholy, which is quickly overshadowed by his misanthropic optimism. . . . While his ears are open to just about any subject matter, race politics is often a recurring theme.

Back there in Kenner, Louisiana, one mile away from the airport, in a small brick house at 329 Webster Street, I can't think of a happier time. As Father was away working and I was truly ambivalent about (and totally unaware of) what was going on, I primarily remember him in terms of his disciplinary actions and educational guidance. As for music, I honestly don't remember a single rehearsal or hearing him practice. I remember Lu and Charlie's nightclub though. Not the music.[25]

MBOYA

Mboya Kenyatta Marsalis was born October 1, 1970. Shortly after his second birthday, Mboya's parents noted that he was talking less and less. There followed many trips to various doctors, only to have it determined that he was autistic.

It is immediately noticed that he is adored (and loved) by his entire family. Mboya reflects contentment and gentleness at all times. He enjoyed working with his music therapist, Dr. Darlene Brooks, for approximately six years. Dr. Brooks, a Loyola University professor, was most fascinated with Mboya's ability to participate in the family music-making, despite the absence of verbal skills. As mother Dolores points out, "Mboya is very special. He is the driving force of this family. He causes us all to realize that no one is perfect. All of us have some imperfections."[26]

JASON

Son Jason Ignatius Marsalis was born March 4, 1977, and is today considered the most talented by all of his brothers. He received a toy set of drums when he was three years old. At age five, he began studying the violin in the Suzuki string program through the public schools. He also studied violin privately and was a member of the New Orleans All-City Orchestra and Strings on Saturday Morning.

Jason moved with his parents to Richmond, Virginia, in 1986. He attended the John P. Cary Elementary School, and participated in the Richmond Sinfonietta and the Richmond Youth Orchestra. Returning to New Orleans in 1989, he lost interest in the violin and began concentrating on percussion instruments, specifically the tympani. He played tympany in the New Orleans All-City Orchestra, studied with the legendary drummer James Black, and at age seven began sitting in with his father's group that appeared regularly at Snug Harbor. He played frequently with his older brother Delfeayo and performed with Delfeayo on his senior recital at Berklee in 1986. Jason played on occasion with Branford and Wynton and played his first complete job with jazz violinist Joseph Kennedy in 1987.

He auditioned for NOCCA and was of course accepted. The summer months of 1993 and 1994 were spent studying orchestral techniques at the Eastern Music Festival in North Carolina. Jason became equally at home with symphony orchestras, jazz orchestras, chamber groups, or jazz combos. He continues to play professional engagements with his father, Ellis, and pianist Marcus Roberts, and frequently fronts his own group.

Dr. David Swanzy was successful in obtaining an interview with Jason for this book on March 3, 1998, at Loyola University. A few questions were asked, but basically Jason simply talked to Swanzy. Both Swanzy and Jason would leave the transcribing to me. Said Jason:

> Wynton bought my first set of drums when I was about six years old. Around age seven, I began sitting in with my father—playing three or four numbers with his group. We talked a lot, always about education. He was always concerned with teaching, not necessarily about music. His concerns were with getting information to the right people.
>
> His concern was that I have a vision—a philosophy. Why am I doing something. For example, at registration, my roommate and I were talking. He was concerned with how much credit he would get, what grade he would get. I was concerned with what I was going to learn; what am I going to gain.

My father always had the answer. When I decided that the violin was no longer the instrument of choice and decided on drums, he had the answer in terms of teachers. First it was Lee Beach, and then Jim Atwood. He always steered me in the right direction. He suggested Eastern Music Festival, saying "I think this would be good for you; why not check it out." He made strong suggestions, but never pressured any of us. He simply said, "This is something to think about." All my musician brothers had been to Eastern Music Festival.

He has tremendous respect for classical music, as do my brothers and I. Of course it took a long time for my father to understand classical music. He was not taught properly. Teachers had this attitude; they talked down to jazz musicians. I think it was when he began teaching at NOCCA that he figured it all out.

I think Wynton had a lot to do with the change of attitude. When he was on the Grammy Awards program, he played the fourth movement of Hummel's Trumpet Concerto, followed by a jazz tune with his quintet (1984). Jazz musicians weren't supposed to be able to play classical music. Of course by the time I was growing up, attitudes were changing. I would encounter that arrogance only occasionally. That attitude is dying out now.

Dr. Swanzy, in preparation for completing the interview, asked Jason if he could say just a few things about his dad specifically. "He is a teacher," answered Jason.

I can recall a situation where a University of New Orleans student was doing a documentary on my dad. He was interviewing me and Delfeayo, asking each of us what we thought of our father. Teacher or player? I said instantly, "A teacher." Delfeayo insisted, "A player" and asked of me, "Do you want to be seen as a teacher or someone who is really playing?" Delfeayo wanted him to move to New York. I played a lot with his trio. It was as if he was teaching all the time.

He is not really excited because he doesn't see himself as a major voice as a player. Once he [my dad] said something to me about marching bands. He insists that more could be done. He suggested that I consider writing out something for the marching band; have it published.[27]

DEAR DOLORES

Patriarch Ellis Marsalis appeared on radio station WBGO out of Newark, N.J., on April 26, 1996, the morning of his and Branford's performance at Town Hall (N.Y.C.). The two were on a short tour, publicizing the recently released CD "Loved Ones" (Columbia), which is devoted to the "romantic effect of ladies upon American songwriters." Ellis included on the CD his composition "Dear Dolores," dedicated to and inspired by his wife. During the radio broadcast, he performed "Dear Dolores" and offered this commentary:

> Dolores is a constant supporter of the music and of all the family. But to say that she was a supporter is kind of mild. If it wasn't for Dolores, there wouldn't have been any of us. The concept of mothering and nurturing is not too well spelled out in this country. What we get is an unfair substitute for the reality of what that job is. Sort of like—the most important non-paying job that there is. There are probably not enough adjectives and accolades to really describe it. In the earlier years of our marriage, my focus and concentration on trying to deal with this music very often caused me some shortsightedness of seeing actually how fantastic a job my wife was doing and how much support was really there. Without a doubt, she is the glue that held it all together.[28]

I met with Dolores on June 26, 1997, at the Marsalis residence. We had met twice previously and had talked by telephone on several occasions. It was obvious that I was in the presence of a very intelligent and articulate woman, a strong human being (she would have to be), self-motivated and self-directed. Let me add that she is also very attractive.

Born April 13, 1937, Dolores Mary Ferdinand graduated from Grambling State University, having majored in home economics. While in college, she sang for a brief period with the university's jazz ensemble. She completed her high school work at St. Mary's Academy, an all-girl's school. "I and Ellis met at Lincoln Beach, when I was seventeen years of age. We married when he returned from the service in 1958."[29]

When I met with Dolores in late June (1997), she had only recently returned from a trip to France, visiting Paris and Normandy. According to Dolores, "this was quite a spiritual experience." Her mother, Leona Ferdinand, spent a lot of time in residence with the Ellis Marsalis family. She accompanied the family to Richmond, Virginia. Dolores had two brothers (one is deceased); the father abandoned the family when Dolores was nine months old. Whereas there was no music in Ellis's background, there was quite a bit on Dolores's side: Related to her mother were violinist/bassist Wellman Braud and the Eugenes. On her father's side was the clarinetist Alphonse Picou. Both Braud and Picou were well-established musicians.

Since I had lived and worked in the Richmond area for many years (1966–1983, primarily as a member of the Richmond Symphony, but also as artist-in-residence, Richmond Public Schools), I was curious about Dolores's reaction to the city. She said,

> At first I didn't like it. There was such a contrast between Richmond and New Orleans. I found it to be interesting once I got into it. You know that I attended graduate school there—Virginia Commonwealth University, School of Social Work. I made many friends.
>
> It was a good situation for Ellis. Maybe he has learned to appreciate himself a little more. Dr. Murry DePillars, dean of the School of Fine Arts, went out on a limb for Ellis. He tried to do something that had never been done before. Ellis's current position at the University of New Orleans is also rewarding. He enjoys his work.
>
> Ellis has said that I am the one who held it all together. This may be true, but at everyone else's expense. I am now sixty years old and I am still with the problems. Being married to Ellis and mothering six sons has not been easy. When the kids were younger, I sought to keep them involved with constructive things. At times I think I must have been overbearing.[30]

But it is all in the family—and what a family it is.

The Virginia Excursion

$\mathcal{E}$llis Marsalis kept the jazz tradition alive in New Orleans, through his own music making and through that of his students. Though all left the city (as did their predecessors), "it was Ellis's leaving that caused eyebrows to be raised. . . .[He had become] a fixture in the Crescent City."[1] While New Orleans wept, Richmond smiled. Wrote Richmond, Virginia's, leading art critic (Clarke Bustard), "Marsalis's Tenure May Forge Musical Link for City."

On June 10, 1986, the *Richmond News Leader* announced that Ellis Marsalis, New Orleans jazz pianist, would teach jazz the following year at Virginia Commonwealth University (VCU). He and his wife had visited the university and Richmond in early May, at which time the deal was sealed. Dr. Richard Koehler, chairman of the department of music, indicated that Marsalis would hold a state-endowed chair, the Commonwealth Professorship in Music, for one year, renewable.

Since mid-June 1986, announcements of Ellis's arrival in Richmond were frequent in the local newspapers. Of particular interest was a Sunday feature article in the Tidewater paper—the *Daily Break* (the *Virginian/Ledger-Star*). The focus was on Virginia Commonwealth University ("An 'A' for the Arts"); the feature was Ellis Marsalis.

VCU's School of the Arts is composed of twelve degree-granting departments and 2,334 students. It has the nation's largest undergraduate sculpture department and an award-winning jazz orchestra. On this scene would arrive Ellis Marsalis, who believes in fundamentals. "I think too often we leave out fundamentals and get involved in exotic activities."[2]

Impressed with what Virginia Commonwealth University was already offering in the area of jazz, Ellis Marsalis felt that his joining the faculty was to expand a program already moving in the right direction—toward Berklee (Boston) or North Texas State (Denton, Texas).

My understanding of what they want me to do at Virginia Commonwealth is have me tailor-make a jazz program for the music department. . . . I won't have to gig to make ends meet. I do now. They do expect me to play because the profile I present is an asset to the school. And I have a chance to do some national-type gigs.[3]

Accompanying Ellis and Dolores would be the two younger of the six children (Mboya and Jason) and Dolores's mother (Leona Ferdinand). The patriarch had become frustrated with New Orleans; the number of "enthusiasts for jazz" had diminished, and the city's musical priorities were changing.

Ellis was in his eleventh year as coordinator of jazz at the New Orleans Center for Creative Arts, the city's high school for the arts. Marsalis had shepherded many of the nation's leading jazz artists at NOCCA (including his sons Wynton and Branford). He was now being referred to as the "godfather of jazz education," though New Orleans youth appeared to have lost interest in playing jazz. As Marsalis explained:

I had one class that had diminished to one female who was 12 years old . . . I had nobody in the jazz ensemble class. I had two bass players and an English kid playing guitar who showed up sometimes. And a drummer who flunked out.[4]

His salary was less than $25,000.

Most artists have at some point in their lives reached a similar point of frustration. And when an opportunity to make adjustments presented itself, they took advantage of it. Ellis was at the "need for change" stage; VCU presented an excellent opportunity. If this meant leaving New Orleans, so be it.

As recently as April 1984, the New Orleans Arts Council had honored the family as "collective keepers of a musical flame who made outstanding musical contributions to New Orleans and the world." In early June 1986, the city was saddened as word circulated that the head of the city's premier jazz family was leaving to accept a position at a university in Richmond, Virginia.

Shirley Trusty Corey, supervisor of arts and education for New Orleans public schools, said, "We're sad he's leaving. He's been a vital and indispensable force in the development of NOCCA's music department." Personnel director for the school system Felix James said, "We were sick at heart" when Marsalis came in to resign. Harwood "Woody" Koppel (another New Orleans public school administrator) said, "What a loss it is. He has been such a generous teacher who has nurtured so many promising young musicians."[5]

Virginia Commonwealth University is the institution that incorporates the Medical College of Virginia, houses a strong School of Social Work (that Dolores Marsalis attended), has a respectable visual arts program within the School of Arts, and in 1986, had several good jazz bands (but not a jazz program). Dean of the School of Arts was graphic artist and painter Dr. Murry DePillars, a jazz lover and enthusiast. He was also a superb and well-respected administrator.

I made every effort to contact Dr. DePillars for information for this book. Although unsuccessful, I did find some earlier comments received via correspondence.

> [Ellis's] presence on campus has changed the environment in our Department of Music. He has bridged an enormous gap between our classical and jazz faculty. The faculty are now talking of the importance of classical music in the development of our students majoring in jazz. Ellis is a model teacher and a true diplomat.[6]

DePillars was the chief engineer in bringing about a meeting of minds (and spirits) between Ellis and VCU's top administrators. DePillars had been alerted to Marsalis's availability by a mutual friend. DePillars wanted a strong jazz program and believed that the right person to develop it was Ellis Marsalis. The fact that Ellis was willing to leave New Orleans created an ideal situation, and the timing was just right.

Shortly after Ellis's announcement of his plans to accept an appointment in another city for the next academic year, he departed with his quartet for a month-long tour of the Philippines, Bangkok, Malaysia, and New Zealand, as well as an appearance at the Montreal Jazz Festival. This was followed by two weeks of performances in New York City. *Gambit* writer Ralph Adamo managed to secure a telephone interview in mid-July and quoted Ellis as having said that he had no details about his new job. Adamo reminded us that NOCCA's jazz instructor might have taken a leave of absence for up to three years, "maintaining status and tenure within the New Orleans public school system." Instead, Ellis elected to resign. "I've always lived like that. I don't care about tenure."

After much probing by the writer, including the speculation that New Orleans and its universities had botched things up, Adamo secured from Ellis the admission that moving closer to his four older children (three in New York City and one in Boston) might bring the family together more frequently. He made clear to the journalist that the move was not permanent; they were not selling their home, and he was not burning any bridges

behind him. "I'm not leaving the country; I'm just going from one southern city to another one." [7]

His last concert in the city prior to the move took place at the Orpheum Theater, as a benefit for NOCCA, on July 24, 1986. He played a
solo set, accompanied two ladies that he had frequently accompanied (Germaine Bazzle and Lady BJ), and performed a set with the Ellis Marsalis
Quartet.

Elizabeth Mullener's August 10, 1986, article in the *Times Picayune* (New
Orleans's daily newspaper) carried in bold caption the headline "Marsalis
Will Leave, But His Heart Won't." When asked about the departure, Ellis
indicated that he was taking New Orleans with him.

> I am New Orleans. . . . That's what I am. Everything about me is New Or-
> leans. I was educated here, I taught school here, the music I play was all de-
> veloped here. Besides, I ain't been anywhere to live but Breaux Bridge, and
> that doesn't count.[8]

Ellis would begin work on August 16, fulfilling a one-year appointment as
commonwealth professor of music, a position that might be offered per-
manently at the end of the year. Clarke Bustard wrote of Marsalis's arrival:

> It could turn into the happiest musical development in Richmond in re-
> cent years. . . . Marsalis's presence on the faculty of Virginia Common-
> wealth University and his participation in Richmond's concert scene may
> forge a musical, geographical and personal link of enormous and enticing
> potential . . .[9]

Marsalis made clear that his reason for being in Richmond was because the
administration had developed a support system. "In Richmond, jazz venues
are established, audiences have been built and the tradition and importance
of jazz is respected. One needs to understand that jazz is not an island."[10]

Though Ellis was noncommittal about his real reasons for leaving or
plans for returning, wife Dolores volunteered:

> We'll be back. . . Ellis is going to get sick of Virginia. . . . [He] has a need to
> be appreciated and paid for what he knows and what he does, . . . All men
> need this, even more than women. There's something about being paid
> properly—it's part of their manhood. If you're serious enough about your art
> to say "this is what I'm going to devote my life to," then you want to get
> paid enough to feel respectable about it.[11]

Dolores pointed out that though the departure had something to do with students and something to do with money, the element of renewal was important. Dolores firmly believed that the move was spiritual and highly personal. "It's like you've got to prove something to yourself, something that you don't prove to anyone else."[12] History proved that Dolores's assessment was absolutely correct.

The state of Virginia utilized his talents and skills and publicized his availability. Hanover Public Schools, with a grant from the Virginia Commission for the Arts and the National Endowment for the Arts, had its first ever musician-in-residence program. For a period of two weeks, Ellis met with Hanover students in elementary and junior and senior high schools, holding workshops, demonstrating, and lecturing. At the end of the two weeks, Ellis would lead a jazz ensemble of twenty-three students from two high schools, in concert on the campus of Randolph Macon College (Ashland, Virginia).

The master teacher met with high school band students in all of Henrico County's high schools, for example, Highland Springs, Tucker, Hermitage, Henrico, Godwin, and Freeman. The county's music specialist was amazed at Marsalis's ability to establish such an excellent rapport with the involved students. Months later, he returned to do a music seminar for the county's band directors. His topic was always music in the broader scheme of things, with emphasis on jazz and career possibilities within the field.

At the end of Ellis's first year, his contract was renewed. He had returned to New Orleans only once—late August 1987. *Times Picayune* journalist Betty Guillard alerted the public to the "musical maven's" return, but he stayed only for a brief visit with friends, family, and students (after a tour of Japan). He was joined on the return trip by Mrs. Marsalis, who had spent the summer in New Orleans.

Approaching the close of his second year (1987–1988), letters from VCU's president informed him that the board of visitors had approved his promotion to the rank of professor and that, having successfully completed a probationary period, his position was now tenured, both effective July 1, 1988. Obviously his presence and service were appreciated and respected; renewal was now his.

Children in Hopewell's (Virginia) Minority Achievement Program also received a visit from master teacher Marsalis. At Carter G. Woodson High School, he sought to explain to students the value of education. These students were "at risk," but Marsalis had no problem telling them that "talents do not lie only in areas highly respected in society, such as law, medicine or engineering. Other avenues, such as the arts, also offer career opportunities."[13]

Marsalis had a powerful sense of mission—fostering and nurturing the music. His desire was to pass it along to the next generation. He believed that he could be a full-time performer, and that if he ever left New Orleans, New York City would be his destination. Now the Big Apple he would leave to younger performers. "Teaching in Richmond seemed just right."[14]

While in Richmond, Ellis was successful in hosting a program for the National Radio Series, showcasing New Orleans jazz. The thirteen-part radio series, titled "Jazztown," focused on contemporary New Orleans jazz and aired nationwide. A year earlier (while still a New Orleans resident), he was host of the New Orleans radio program "Milestones," which was national in scope.

But after three years, New Orleans would recapture his heart. Once more, the ideal situation had presented itself. He would depart for the city during the summer of 1989 and become founding director and professor of music in a jazz studies program at University of New Orleans (UNO). No application was filed. The job was created specifically for him.

In New Orleans, Ellis was viewed as one who kept the jazz tradition alive and one who fathered a new generation of jazzmen. They left the city one by one and moved on to noteworthy musical careers elsewhere, all before Ellis.

> But it was Ellis's leaving that caused the eyebrows to be raised. . . . He was a fixture in the Crescent City. . . . When Ellis Marsalis left it was a shock, a slap in the face, a renunciation.[15]

Dated December 12, 1988, the Christmas prior to Ellis's final departure from Richmond, the following was directed to me personally:

> As my three-year tenure at VCU draws to a close, I reflect on the move; the anxiety (age, distance, culture shock) that accompanied the experience did not set in until I started to think in terms of "What if . . . ?" While it seemed an adventure to me, it was a nightmare to Dolores. While I did not at any time think it was a wrong move, being away from New Orleans helped me to see possible solutions much clearer. It now seems as if it was a gigantic plan with predestined results. A plan in which I was a player in a game that I only thought I knew the rules. Now it seems that going back to New Orleans is as much a part of the "game" as having left.

I am writing you from the Quality Inn in Charleston, S.C. Mboya and I have come here by train for a special treatment for his autism. On Friday, Dolores is going to drive from Richmond with Jason and her mother to meet us here and we will continue on to New Orleans.[16]

Then the real move. After three years, returning to New Orleans meant holding a $1 million endowed chair at the University of New Orleans, $600,000 to be donated by Louisiana Coca-Cola Bottling Company, Ltd., and $400,000 coming from the state's board of regents. His plans were to try to establish a model program for the serious study of jazz music. He wanted to create a training ground for a pool of New Orleans musicians, because there were so few in the city. Many were leaving the city or engaging in some other activity.

He also planned to establish a visiting-artist series, attracting such jazz performers as James Moody and Dizzy Gillespie. The university's dean of liberal arts wanted UNO to become the premier jazz studies program in the country, stating, "I think we have the right man for the job."[17] President and chief executive officer of Louisiana Coca-Cola said, "This marks the return of the most creative jazz teacher in America to his home city of New Orleans."[18] Chancellor Gregory O'Brian had plans for making the university one of the nation's most competitive, and a jazz studies program was essential to that plan.

His farewell Richmond appearance took place on March 10, 1989. It was a solo event, much to the satisfaction of his audience. He presented an overview of jazz composition along with his command of it.

> Marsalis was the essence of cool as he strolled to a dusty grand in VCU's packed Performing Arts Center. . . . [He] is a master of technique and interpretation. Last night, he used the whole keyboard, played with tempos and showed full familiarity with jazz piano, barely pausing three beats, after applause, between tunes.[19]

DePillars indicated that "Ellis did a yeoman's job at VCU." Music department chairman Richard Koehler indicated that he would be sorry to see him leave.

> His approach was less academic. . . . His approach was, "This is what it's like out there in the trenches, folks." He's been doing it year in and year out. Chapter one in the book doesn't tell you that.[20]

Reminiscences:
Friends and Professional Associates

$\mathcal{A}$dmiration and respect for "Marsalis the Elder" goes far beyond my personal recognition. Hence it is that I asked a select group of individuals to address the subject. The eighteen respondents wrote of Marsalis's pianistic skills and elegant style, his intelligence, his scholarship, his integrity, and his improvisational thinking. In addition to developing as a pianist, one wrote of his experience with the cello; another, of his experience with the clarinet and tenor saxophone. All addressed his outstanding tutorial skills. Following is my request:

Dear [fill in the blank]:

I am currently working on a biography of Ellis Marsalis. For a chapter devoted to "Friends and Professional Associates Recall," Ellis has provided me with your name as one who he believes would be able (and willing) to "shed some light" on the subject. . . .

Please be kind enough to share with me and a reading public any and everything that you feel is appropriate. Length is of no import. Also, feel free to validate this request by checking with Ellis.

Your response is greatly anticipated. Please forward same in the enclosed stamped envelope.

Sincerely yours,

D. Antoinette Handy

DR. FREDERICK TILLIS

Dr. Frederick Tillis, composer, jazz saxophonist, poet, and director of the Fine Arts Center at the University of Massachusetts at Amherst (recently retired) shared these thoughts about Ellis Marsalis: "A book on Ellis should be very interesting reading and will be a significant contribution to the literature and related pedagogy of jazz." Personalizing his opinions, Tillis further wrote:

> I have the highest respect and admiration for him. As a pianist and musician, he is a master of the art of jazz. He is a very lyrical pianist who also swings intensely with grace.
>
> Ellis and I have had conversations on various occasions on music and a range of other subjects. He brings an incisive intelligence and a firm philosophical perspective regarding various aspects of culture in America. Marsalis is very conscious of the many subtleties and degrees of depth that the many ethnic and diverse groups outside of the African-American culture bring to the interpretation of jazz and other forms of music. Needless to say, I have the highest respect for the integrity and commitment of Ellis Marsalis as an important musician in American culture.

DAN MORGENSTERN

Dan Morgenstern, jazz historian, author, and director of the Institute of Jazz Studies at Rutgers, the State University of New Jersey, offered a brief but profound statement on the subject:

> The name of Ellis Marsalis would be writ large in the annals of jazz even if he had not fathered his truly remarkable brood, for he is a pianist of uncommon elegance and style, and a remarkable teacher and proselytizer who has done much to make the music thrive. He is the veritable incarnation of a gentleman and a scholar.

SHIRLEY TRUSTY COREY

Shirley Trusty Corey, New Orleans Center of Creative Arts founder, hired Ellis to begin a jazz program at the center in 1974. Ellis was the first officially designated teacher in the Orleans Parish school system to develop and teach a jazz curriculum. Of his involvement, she wrote:

The best teachers illuminate and motivate. As philosopher and teacher, Ellis Marsalis shares his innate musicality in a style that not only teaches skills but propels his students to continually search for the extension of musical forms and of themselves.

DR. JOSEPH B. BUTTRAM

Dr. Joseph B. Buttram, former dean of the College of Music at Loyola University in New Orleans and director, School of Music at Ball State University (recently retired), met Ellis in the late 1960s at Lu and Charlie's on Rampart Street. Much to his pleasant surprise, he encountered "some 'mainstream' jazz, just like in the Village!" These are his observations:

I had heard nothing like this in New Orleans before. . . . There he was, along with a rhythm section and one horn. The ensemble was excellent. My friend and I stayed until around 2:00 A.M., just listening. I went home thrilled that I had found a real contemporary jazz artist right here in the home of traditional jazz. (I had become a little disappointed that I had not found more contemporary and "mainstream" jazz.)

I returned repeatedly to the same venue to hear Ellis and others. I managed to say hello, speak with him briefly from time to time, and gradually got to know him.

I was starting a new graduate program. Ellis was looking for a way to get an advanced degree without leaving the city; so I quickly invited him to consider our new program. Before long, he was enrolled, in attendance, and (wonder of wonders) sitting in my classes.

Verifying what so many others have said, this educator wrote:

He is a real intellect—a fine scholar, philosopher and broadly educated generally. And, this is in addition to his superb musicianship and proven pedagogical expertise! What a "find" for Loyola! With him came a number of other fine musicians and students and we enjoyed a virtual "hotbed" of musical and scholarly activity.

Ellis often brought to campus members of his family—two absolutely charming young men (Branford and Wynton) along with his stunning wife! Though I left the city in the mid-70s, Ellis and I continued to be in touch and I followed his career as well as those of his sons.

Ellis has enjoyed unusual success both as a performer and teacher. He provided the milieu and instruction for his phenomenal sons and has attracted as many other fine young musicians to study with him as anyone in the world. Why this is the case, I do not know but will speculate. Ellis represents about as completely as any single individual the history of jazz in our country and in many ways, the history of the assimilation of the varied peoples in our culture. He represents that combination of characteristics that are sometimes used to describe jazz—intuition and intellect, freedom and form, individual expression within social context, fixed and variable pitch, polyrhythmic structure, and so on. He also represents in a most general and profound way the best of outcomes from the blending of peoples and their cultural traditions.

This is why he is such a great teacher. He knows in an intimate way and in many, many dimensions. He "senses" and he "understands" why the music is as it is and why it has to be learned the way it is learned. I am so very proud to have known him and even prouder to be able to call him my friend.

GERRI M. ELIE

I met Gerri M. Elie, associate vice president for academic affairs at Dillard University, when she came to Washington, D.C., to serve as a lay panelist on one of the music program's panels at the National Endowment for the Arts. Since both she and I were from New Orleans, we conversed extensively about the city and one of her favorite sons, Ellis Marsalis. In response to my request for a recollection, she wrote:

I met Ellis for the first time when we entered our freshman year at Dillard University. I remember a tall, lanky young man who walked with a slight lope and seemed to be perpetually humming a tune or beating out a rhythm on any object that happened to be around. For the most part, he was not one of the gang, not a "groupie"; but while he pretty much kept to himself (or his small band of followers), he did not seem at all unfriendly—just distant and absorbed in his thoughts.

After the initial "getting acquainted" sessions and registration, I re-discovered Ellis in the band room. He played the clarinet in Dillard's twelve piece band under the direction of Dr. David Buttolph. It wasn't long before I learned that my meager reading of the notes and producing some acceptable sounds on the clarinet, I fell far short of the beautiful tones that came from Ellis Marsalis and his best friend Roger Dickerson.

The one thing that I remember most is that both Roger and Ellis were very patient with me, a third chair clarinet player, struggling to keep my "Dillard Activity Scholarship." The terms of my agreement included playing in the band. So Ellis spent many hours helping me to keep up.

While other guys were out chasing girls on campus, I would often find Ellis alone (or with Roger) playing some strange tune on the piano in one of the practice rooms. He always hummed as he played and seemed to cover more notes on the piano with his long fingers than anyone our age could imagine. As students, we gathered around him to pay homage to a sound that we did not quite understand. But we knew that it was different and so was Ellis.

I have very little recall of Ellis in any of my other classes. I can only recall him in Coss Hall, the old music building.

After graduation, Ellis plied his trade in small joints with groups of jazz musicians as he learned from the so-called "masters." While most of us were doing the jitterbug and listening to Louis Jordan, the old Temptations and other rhythm and blues greats, Ellis was championing jazz idols like Thelonius Monk and Erroll Garner who made little sense to me.

I remember distinctly Ellis's attempt to start a jazz club in New Orleans after traveling around the country and seeing how few places catered to really good jazz clubs (with the exception of New York City). His father cooperated in this venture by adding a new section to his already existing motel. Our gang of young marrieds traveled the Old River Road to Shrewsbury to hear our schoolmate and friend.

While Ellis also brought top-notch entertainers each time I visited, I realized that l) New Orleans was not ready to support such a venture and 2) the club was located in Jefferson Parish on the Old River Road where few white people dared to venture, even if they liked jazz. This was of course before integration.

I can also remember feeling so sad when I heard that the club might not make it. Later I learned that it had closed and Ellis was once again out playing on the road. He never gave up—never seemed discouraged or unhappy with his life. I thought of him as a jazz messenger long before I heard of Art Blakey's group by that name.

HAROLD R. BATTISTE JR.

Saxophonist Harold R. Battiste Jr. is Ellis's coworker in the jazz studies program at the University of New Orleans. He is also one to whom Ellis gives thanks for having provided him with his first real jazz lesson. I selected Harold to serve on one of the National Endowment for the Arts' panels in Washington, D.C. He graciously provided the following:

My most vivid memory is of a young cat with a smile . . . more like a grin . . . that seemed like he was having more fun than the rest of the musicians. Maybe he was, because he had "golden ears" which were aided by "magic fingers." He could hear beautiful ways to voice music and his hands seemed to find the right keys to express that beauty.

Of course all that came in time. I knew Ellis first as a high school tenor saxophone player with the "Groovy Boys." In my senior year at Dillard University, Ellis entered as a freshman music student. It may have been during this time that he began to discover himself as a jazz pianist.

In 1956 Ellis and I went to Los Angeles with drummer Ed Blackwell. The sojourn ultimately resulted in a recording opportunity for the "Original American Jazz Quintet." This group evolved over the next few years into the "Ellis Marsalis Quartet" which still represents the best of New Orleans modern jazz.

I have a deep love and appreciation for Ellis's musical spirit and do not have words that express that . . . I'd rather just play something with him.

VICTOR GOINES

One of Ellis's many talented (and successful) students who has moved on to bigger and better things is Victor Goines, a private student of the professor. A professional musician (saxophone and clarinet) and a native of New Orleans, he considers Ellis Marsalis to be a mentor, a teacher, a colleague, and a friend. During my phone conversation with him, the remembrances flowed freely:

> There is absolutely no one who I would stop anything for, as I would for Ellis. Anything this man suggested that I do was always the best decision for my career development. I followed him to Richmond, wherefrom I received my masters degree. He is unselfish, to the extent that when he plays with students, he has to remind himself that an audience also wants to hear him. He is always teaching, 24/7, 365 days of the year. Ellis understands the music. I began playing with him in 1984, in a quartet that he assembled. When Ellis returned to New Orleans (following his stay at Virginia Commonwealth University), I moved on to New York. I taught at Loyola University for one year and most recently, at Florida A&M University in Tallahassee. Around it all, I am a member of the Lincoln Center Jazz Orchestra. (Where Wynton Marsalis is music director.)

Enthusiasm for a teacher? Victor has enough to share with a few others.

CLIFFORD V. JOHNSON

If my memory serves me correctly, I met Clifford V. Johnson during the course of one of his visits to a college where I was teaching (when he was affiliated with the Institute for Services to Education). We met again during the World's Fair (1984)—Louisiana World Exposition "I've Known Rivers," Afro-American Pavilion. Formerly vice president for Development at Dillard University (Johnson and Ellis's alma mater), Johnson has been a friend of Ellis's since their college days (early 1950s). Johnson pointed out that most impressive to him about Ellis Marsalis is his true love of music and that, with a family and a full-time teaching job, he still manages to make the gigs and develop his talents. He further wrote:

My earliest recollections of Ellis Marsalis as a youngster go back to the late 1940s, when his father ran an Esso service station on South Claiborne Avenue near Louisiana Avenue in New Orleans. But I really got to know him when we were students at Dillard University. He was a year ahead of me. Ellis and his inseparable companion Roger "Dickie" Dickerson played gigs in the French Quarter. In campus bull sessions, Ellis often talked about after-hours life on the other side of the color bar, the risque happenings he saw but didn't see. Ellis offered vivid descriptions of a forbidden and dangerous world.

In 1953, we were accepted into the Crescent Club of Phi Beta Sigma Fraternity, Inc. Roger, a Sigma, probably influenced Ellis to join. I probably did it because of my admiration for both of them. Roger was Dean of Pledges. I actually believe he turned the screw a notch or two more than needed so as not to be accused of favoritism. Ellis and I "crossed the burning sands" in the spring of 1954, covering as best we could one another's (sore) butts. Fraternal humiliation took place both on and off campus. But we survived.

There was a snack bar located in the Student Union Building. Its most attractive feature was a bulky, brightly-lit jukebox, loaded with lots of jazz recordings. Ellis had a deal working with the man who regularly stocked the records. Many of the commuter students spent time between classes and at lunchtime gathered around the box, drawing inspiration from the latest Miles, Monk, Parker, Diz and other mid-fifties bebop genuises. Ellis and Roger were my "Jazz 101" professors and Dillard's box was one of the best learning resources in town. There was also a listening area in the Rosenwald Hall, administration building library, and Ellis obviously had clout with the librarian, because among the perfunctory classical selections were current releases by Dave Brubeck, Stan Kenton and Duke Ellington orchestras. When you listened to music with him, you could count on receiving a lecture on various Kenton arranging talents, the technical prowess of Maynard Ferguson, or Ellington's compositional brilliance.

Ellis, his cohort Roger, and other music majors made up a small pep band that rocked the stands at home football games. A flatted fifth-filled jazz run on a music department piano would get you reported to the dean—accused of breaking the university's instrument. A rebellious, "never let 'em see you sweat" kind of guy, Ellis would play anyway. Ironically, I was to see virtually the same temperament years later, in his son Branford. As Yogi Berra is said to have uttered, "deja vu all over again."

Over the next twenty years, my contacts with him were spotty. I recall during visits home in the late '60s hearing Ellis play at Al Hirt's on Bourbon Street (post-apartheid). In the '70s, I heard him play in a variety of small and large settings: Lu and Charlies, the Hyatt Regency Hotel, Tyler's Beer Garden, and at the New Orleans Jazz and Heritage Festival.

The hippest musicians hung out at Lu and Charlies. Ellis let Wynton, then barely in his early teens, sit in with the band. Obvious was Ellis's easy-going teaching style. He never seemed to press his boys to play. If they did, o.k., if not, o.k. The rest is history. Seeing Jason, Ellis's talented youngest son, sit in with his father in recent years, beginning at an even earlier age than Wynton, brings back memories of the very special nature of the father/son/master/apprentice relationship Ellis had with his sons.

Ellis frequently philosophized about his favorite subjects: music, politics, and the general (usually bad) state of the union. A perk I always looked forward to when going to Ellis's set at Tylers was seeing Wynton whenever he was in town. Usually they played standards, and Ellis, the ever obliging father-teacher, would encourage the very attentive younger Marsalis to delve deeper into the inner mysteries of tunes obviously bound for the latter's future performances and recordings.

Ten years later, when I was senior program associate in humanities at the Institute for Services to Education (ISE), Washington, D.C., I asked Roger, then my principal music consultant, to help put together an outline on the evolution of jazz and other secular Afro-American music. The ISE organization offered technical assistance to clusters of historically black colleges that were attempting to make their curricula more relevant to the experiences of black students. We had the daunting task of developing curriculum manuals for teachers whose educational backgrounds included little or no information on the cultural products of our (black) people. Roger asked Ellis to work on the jazz section of an inclusive outline. Ellis responded by producing an annotated outline on the history of jazz, which offered as succinct and straight-forward a tribute to the monumental role of blacks in defining music in America as you'd find anywhere. Twenty years later, it has withstood the test of time.

As a part of the educational activities of the 1984 Louisiana World Exposition "I've Known Rivers" Afro-American Pavilion, Ellis and noted musician, educator and television personality Billy Taylor did a lecture-demonstration illustrating the history of jazz. It was clearly a crowd pleaser and an overall success. They respected one another. So palpable was the chemistry between them we asked that they do a benefit piano duo concert, this time with two grand pianos, in a space more suited to a concert. They consented.

The concert was an artistic *tour de force* by two giants of the instrument. The Marsalis/Taylor duo was filmed for cable television. I believe that video program was distributed nationally.

DONALD M. MARQUIS

Donald M. Marquis, editor of the New Orleans Jazz Club's publication *The Second Line,* met Ellis in the late 1960s. Here are his memories of the man:

Ellis occasionally sat in for the pianist in Louis Cottrell's Band at Dixieland Hall on Bourbon Street. When in 1973 this hall closed, activities moved on to Crazy Shirley's, on the corner of Bourbon and St. Peter, another traditional jazz venue. . . . The more I listened to him, the more I began to appreciate what Ellis was doing.

He went on to work in education and I published a book that gave me some credibility. In time, we met again, primarily serving on the same committee. Ellis always had ideas to contribute, but there were times when the first appeal to him was, "Can you get Wynton and Branford to help us out?" I don't know Ellis's true reaction, but it turned me off. Such a pity that these committee members thought that that could be his only contribution.

The author of *In Search of Buddy Bolden* (1978) concluded his comments by writing: "I think Ellis has a handle on jazz, from its earliest days to what is happening now and perhaps in the future. He is a great teacher, as well as a great musician."

JOHN T. SCOTT

These comments were offered by John T. Scott, artist (sculptor) and educator, recipient of the John D. and Catherine T. MacArthur Foundation's "genius" award, and one of New Orleans's most respected artists:

I find writing about a friend a difficult task, for I know that I cannot be objective. Where Ellis is concerned, I know that I am biased, for his friendship is so close that I see him through the eyes of a friend and admirer.

Sometime ago, I lost count as to how long we have been friends. It has been a long time I know. We met on Xavier University's campus when he taught there. Soon we were team teaching. This we did whenever we had the opportunity. I was first drawn to him by his openmindedness and curiosity. He was not the kind of musician that would dismiss a non–musician's question; instead, he would attempt to help you understand the musician's point of view. Soon we began to compare the commonalities between our disciplines, finding that they and we had an awful lot in common.

Scott offers these firsthand observations of Ellis's broadness and objectivity:

> We worked together on a number of projects, from teaching to art installations, to conceptual ideas for the interior designs for an airport based on an eight bar composition he wrote. All worked perfectly. The improvisational thinking he brings to his music he also brought to the collective creative process. Ellis understands that the major difference between music and other creative forms is language, not ideas.

Scott says that a conversation with Ellis is a creative experience for him, because of how he is able to bounce off ideas "without the fear of feeling stupid." From his students I have the understanding that he brings the above attitudes to his teaching. To summarize:

> Ellis is a person who is generous with his time, ideas and knowledge, and is always open to new ideas. Willing to disagree at times, but never disagreeable or disrespectful. He is an artist that understands the relatedness of the arts that allows each of us to grow. He has so much to teach and I have so much to learn from him.

DR. RALPH R. SIMPSON

Dr. Ralph R. Simpson joined the Dillard University faculty in 1960 and remained there for six years. Ellis graduated in 1955, joined the Marines, and settled back in New Orleans, only to convince himself that he needed to know more. Wrote Simpson:

> The site was the hallway of Coss Hall of Dillard University, where I was greeted by a strikingly serious young man who humbled me by saying "You must be that cat who is a great organist; who is also heavy in theory." I replied that I was trying to become guilty on both counts. After stating his name, he immediately informed me that he was the brother of Yvette (Eve) who was studying piano with me at the time. He asked if I would coach him in theory? I was extremely curious and asserted, "But you are a music graduate from Dillard!" He interrupted by saying, "But I did not learn a damn thing in theory." I consented to accept him as a private student and presented him with a copy of *Advanced Harmony* by Ottman. I further asked him to

read and work out the exercises in the chapter on diatonic sevenths. He objected saying, "I want to start from scratch—you see, I'm interested in knowing what the hell I'm doing."

Ellis was my first non-traditional student. I, therefore, was not offended by his occasional vulgarity. Furthermore, I was comforted by the fact that his actions gave me license to throw an occasional curse word in his direction.

We launched into our study with vigor: major, minor, gapped, Javanese, Neapolitan, synthetic (you name it) scales. Much later we discussed serialization techniques, etc. This man was a veritable sponge, who stimulated me as much as he was apparently being stimulated. He would ask probing questions, e.g., "Why is it desirable to double the third in a major triad?" This question, for example, gave me an opportunity to talk about the overtone series and acoustics. In summary, the man extracted every ounce of knowledge I had acquired to that point in my existence, and made me validate my recent terminal degree.

Between theory sessions we talked about world news, politics, and education. Indeed, Ellis introduced me to the *Republic*, a publication that dealt with international issues and their impact on world culture and on the plight of mankind.

We worked together for approximately one year. I hasten to add that our busy schedules impacted greatly the frequency of these sessions. I truly cherish my brief association with one of America's shining musical stars.

GEORGE WEIN

One of the fastest responses to my request came from promoter/producer/jazz concert impresario/pianist George Wein. And I had envisioned that this would be one of the responses I would never receive, what with his busy schedule. I was aware that as producer and CEO of the popular New Orleans Jazz and Heritage Festival, interaction with Ellis was certain. Following is Wein's offering:

We met in 1969, when I was working with my band (Red Norvo, Ruby Braff, and Larry Ridley). We were working at the Royal Sonesta Hotel. Ellis was working across the street with Al Hirt's band. Ellis gave a modern inflection to Al Hirt's Dixieland music. It was an interesting combination.

Wynton and Branford were just babies. Ellis and I usually met after hours and had a few drinks. I was always impressed by Ellis's professionalism. At that time, I had no idea that he was such a great teacher. Ellis always worked at the New Orleans Jazz and Heritage Festival which started in 1970. He was considered the best modern pianist in New Orleans. I noticed that he was always more or less a leader of the musicians he worked with. Several years later, when I was building a band for Lionel Hampton for the festival, Ellis picked most of the New Orleans musicians. There was a young trumpet player, approximately 15 or 16 years old, who I was later told was Ellis's son named Wynton.

Now far more knowledgeable of Ellis's stature in the city, Wein pointed out that he was amazed at the job that Ellis does in New Orleans:

> There is a whole school of great young musicians and Ellis Marsalis is their teacher and leader. He has meant as much to the development of the great jazz musicians that have come out of New Orleans in the past decade as anyone. As a true teacher and because of what has happened with these musicians from New Orleans, he has become an important figure in the development of this great American music. Ellis Marsalis has become a giant in a field where great teachers are needed.

DR. LORRAINE WILSON

Former supervisor of music for the New Orleans public schools and one to whom Marsalis reported (in the public schools) was Dr. Lorraine Wilson, now a professor of music at Indiana University in Pennsylvania. She recalled that she and a friend frequented the Marsalis home, primarily to "have fun" with Ellis's younger sister Yvette:

> Frequently I would see Ellis, who played saxophone in Gilbert Academy's High School Band. There were opportunities to hear him practicing, as well as to see him dressed in a beautiful blue and gold uniform prior to a football game. I was so impressed that I dreamed of attending Gilbert Academy and playing in the band. Needless to say, I was disappointed when I heard that this private school closed a year before I was to enroll.

Appointed supervisor of music for the New Orleans public schools in 1978, she had the frequent opportunity to visit, observe, and work collaboratively with Ellis at the New Orleans Center for Creative Arts (NOCCA). "There I observed an astute tutor at work." Of Marsalis's tenure at NOCCA (1974–1986) she wrote:

> He displayed remarkable teaching techniques, approaches, methods and strategies to assure student achievement and success for career goals. Ellis had the ability to motivate students, thereby extending student goals. High expectations were always made known to these talented students through his wisdom, un-

tiring efforts, and contagious enthusiasm. Ellis took the time to teach reasoning and expository skills thereby impacting the cognitive and affective domains of each student. Because he could think creatively, he was able to inspire students to think and perform with a high degree of creativity. He demonstrated excellence in communication skills, clearly articulating a desired professionalism.

This scholar/teacher contributed significantly to jazz studies for the total school curriculum. Ellis had the ability to convey the need for improved curricula, resources, and experiences for students K–12.

I recall the countless hours he provided on curriculum development committees and planning meetings—leadership skills, profound insights and knowledge, all beneficial in developing and revising music curriculum for a school system of 85,000 students. He was also consultant and writer for a very special cultural resources project, chaired by Shirley Trusty Corey, supervisor of arts in education and founder of NOCCA.

During the days of Professional Improvement Programs (PIP), Ellis was a frequent workshop clinician. He demonstrated insight related to strategies, approaches, and resources for integrating jazz studies in general music classes and instrumental music.

Finally, Ellis Marsalis is a master teacher, endowed with intellect and incredible sensitivity for music-making. He is innovative and artistically superior. In addition, he is selfless, accessible, reflective, and concerned about students.

DR. HENRY C. LACEY

Dr. Henry C. Lacey, vice president for academic affairs at Dillard University (Ellis's alma mater), agreed without hesitation to write something about one of his "real heroes." Lacey was familiar with Marsalis's work long before making his acquaintance. He wrote:

I first heard Ellis in the context of his fine quartet, featuring Nat Perrilliat (tenor saxophone), Marshall Smith (bass) and James Black (drums). I was enthralled by the extent to which Marsalis and Company captured the spirit and "vibe" of jazz's most cutting-edge group (John Coltrane's Quartet). A few friends and I frequented a place called The Haven, on Claiborne Street. We believed that Marsalis, Perrilliat, Smith, and Black were in every respect equal to Coltrane, Tyner, Garrison, and Jones.

I continued to follow Marsalis's career, at Lu and Charlie's (a relatively short-lived but important music club of the 1970s). It was in this group that I first heard flutist Kent Jordan, for example. Ellis was also frequently performing with gifted and promising NOCCA students.

Lacey frequently caught Ellis at Tyler's Beer Garden, an uptown bistro that was the leading spot for contemporary jazz in the 1980s. In addition to featuring his sons Wynton and Branford, he often worked with such established artists as Eddie Harris and Nat Adderly:

> Upon the demise of Tyler's, Ellis was given top billing at Snug Harbor, another contemporary jazz club. Several worked with him there who "got it together" under his demanding tutelage, including Victor Goines, Reginald Veal, and his son Jason, all honing their skills with Ellis at Snug Harbor.

Lacey and Marsalis's musical encounters became less frequent, but the two met from time to time for various verbal exchanges:

> I find his catholicity of taste—his concern with promotion of good music, no matter the idiom—most refreshing. I have found him to be a man with a passionate desire to improve our troubled educational system in general. Having nurtured so many confident, creative, productive young artists and citizens, he obviously knows a lot about what works educationally. Perhaps it's time we *really listened* to Ellis Marsalis.

DR. MICHAEL WHITE

The following entry might be categorized as an essay; it is a bit lengthy but absolutely nothing could be sacrificed. Some deletions were considered, but the idea, for the most part, was abandoned, in view of the fact that its content was so enlightening and the writer was so important to New Orleans music. Dr. Michael White, clarinetist, early jazz historian, frequent performer at Lincoln Center (N.Y.C.) with Wynton Marsalis, world traveler with Preservation Hall jazz ensembles, and professor of Spanish at Xavier University (New Orleans), offered the following essay:

> One could not grow up in uptown New Orleans during the seventies without having heard the name Ellis Marsalis. The rhythmic ring of that name could be heard coming from the lips of your high school band director, television announcements of the jazzfest, or weekly radio broadcasts "live from Lu and Charlie's." In some music classes at Xavier University the name Ellis Marsalis evoked fear, because it meant someone who was serious, took no mess off of you, and let you know that there was no "getting over" in his classes. Your friends told you of how he lectured you, made you face your own realities, and told you just what you needed to do to get yourself together. It was obvious that he must have been from another planet because just a direct look from him meant instant exposure of your juvenile resist-

ance to conscious thought and high level learning. Fear! Though you never actually took a class from him, the reports from your friends who did made you wisely run for cover into another aisle at the neighborhood supermarket where you saw the frightening legend all too often.

As the years passed, fear turned into respect as you entered the tough local music scene. He was in his world and you were in yours, but on some level you knew that he must have been extremely tough because he was still out there. He exemplified basic characteristics that every jazz musician who wanted to survive needed: a genuine love of music, faith, perseverance, hard work, a progressive attitude towards study and practice, and a search for a genuine musical identity.

Ellis was into his MODERN JAZZ SCENE and you were into your TRADITIONAL NEW ORLEANS JAZZ SCENE with the really OLD cats, and since these two worlds seemed to differ so vastly in style and musical philosophies, of course you would never come in direct contact with him. I very clearly remember the sense of disbelief which came when I arrived early at the Toulouse Theater to play in the "One Mo' Time" show and learned that Ellis Marsalis was to be our pianist that evening—on the most involved traditional job in town at that time!

Never mind that it was to be his first time doing the show, or that they weren't sure that he had ever seen the music or had heard the show; I immediately reverted back to the fearful student who was consumed with other concerns. Would he play "modern" altered chords and accents that didn't blend with the 1920s show music? Could he play the more rhythmic style of piano that traditional music needed? This time there were no aisles of safety to duck behind. What would he say to me? Would he chastise me for playing an early clarinet jazz style that sounded so very different from what most players under the age of 70 were doing? I thought about the never-ending controversies in jazz on what was considered "hip"; on how some people felt that you were "supposed" to play with bebop overtones because anything else wasn't progressive or "black."

When Ellis walked in, all of my college days' fears were reconfirmed as everything about him seemed to indicate that he had a lot more going on than the rest of us mere mortals. He walked up the dark aisle towards the stage with his head deeply engrossed into a book. At the same time, he listened to music through headphones. Without ever looking up or interrupting his activities, he came up the steps and went behind the curtain that led to the bandstand.

Ellis only had a short time to FIND THE MUSIC SCORES and LOOK OVER THEM before the show began. Ellis adjusted to the show well and played beautifully. During the intermission I looked up all of a sudden to see what I had feared most: Ellis staring at me! It was obvious that he was sizing me up—assessing, making conclusions, and saying to himself "uh huh."

After a few minutes of this silent scenario, an uneasiness had built up in me so much that I heard my mouth utter in his direction: "Is something the matter?" After a few more seconds of head bobbing, Ellis finally broke his silence. He said, "You amaze me." I just knew what was coming next: how the traditional style I was playing was outdated; how it was from "Uncle Tom Music"; how I needed to learn bebop; how it was "wrong" to play like those "old men," etc. Ellis's next line seemed to be a lead-in for the main attack: "I didn't know that they still had people who could play that way." Defensive and apologetic, I told him that I really loved traditional New Orleans jazz and that I didn't know anything about playing modern jazz. Having understood my interpretation of and reaction to his comments, Ellis quickly clarified what he meant: "No, no. I mean that's good. I didn't know that there were any younger blacks that much into that style. Don't worry about trying to play modern. Keep doin' what you're doin. They need that out here."

From that day on, I became a devoted "student" of Ellis Marsalis. The "One Mo' Time" meeting was only the first in a series of incidents that exposed me to the high level of intellect and wisdom that Ellis has. When he has to speak or make decisions, he does so from the perspective of one who sees the big picture. His words are sound; his focus is clear; his words are often profound; his advice often prophetic.

Besides being a great pianist, an inspirational educator, and a successful program director, he is a model of what many of us need to be. He remains a tireless crusader for the cause of jazz. A true artist, Ellis has constantly explored his own creativity. His music speaks to us. It challenges us. It explains things to us that even Ellis couldn't verbalize. In essence, Ellis Marsalis is one of those few truly inspirational and influential people that God has sent to us so that in the midst of our own frivolous wanderings and lack of direction we can begin the course of exploring the potentials of our hopes, dreams, fears, and aspirations.

WILLIAM S. FISHER

William S. Fisher, composer of rock, pop, traditional jazz, rhythm 'n' blues, and orchestral and chamber music, wrote the following of his relationship with Ellis Marsalis:

We met in 1951 when Jackson College (now University) played Dillard University in a football game at Dillard (New Orleans). Jackson College's marching band and Dillard's student-organized band had a jam session after the game, with members of both bands participating. I listened only and Ellis took part by playing the tenor saxophone.

I saw Ellis a year later, at Xavier University (New Orleans), where I was a student. Ellis had a little convertible Studebaker, with a plaid top. Certainly he was the only person who had such a car.

Over the many years, we both grew in the same circles in New Orleans. He used to come around the Dew Drop Club where I played in the house band. He dare not play the rock 'n' roll we were creating; he wanted only to play 1940s Northeast Jazz. Very few gigs were possible playing such music then.

There were many similarities between William Fisher and Ellis Marsalis: both played saxophone and piano; both married girls named Dolores; and both had four boys (at the time). Some years later, when I was teaching at Xavier, Ellis came by and wanted to take cello lessons—out of the blue. I gave him every reason for sticking with the piano, because he had arrived at a point where basic information might hamper his creative instincts. But he insisted. He had talent; he had a good tone and a decent bow arm.

Ellis had no time to practice the exercises and reading got in the way of the bow arm. If he had time to practice, he could have been a fine cellist. But the best sound for cello was in the classical field and I am certain Ellis was made for jazz, to be sure.

ALVIN BATISTE SR.

Outstanding clarinetist (with a specialty in jazz and an international reputation) and Southern University–Baton Rouge professor and director of the university's jazz progam, Alvin Batiste Sr. had much to offer on the subject of Ellis Marsalis:

We were enrolled in the same class at F. P. Richard Elementary School in New Orleans. After graduation, we went to different high schools—I went to Booker T. Washington and Ellis went to Gilbert Academy and later, Gaudet High. We met three years later in a competition held at Southern University. We competed, both performing the Rondo from Mozart's Clarinet Concerto.

After high school graduation, we went to two different universities. I enrolled at Southern University in Baton Rouge and Ellis enrolled at Dillard University. In 1955 Ellis and I began playing together, with Nat Perrilliat, Harold Battiste, Richard Payne, Edward Blackwell and several other musicians. At one time or another, the group included everybody we knew in New Orleans who was influenced by the music of Charlie Parker, Clifford Brown and Horace Silver. We had access to two grand pianos in the African-American community—one was Yvette Marsalis's piano (Ellis's sister) and the other was at the home of Wylene Chatters Heron, my sister-in-law. Ellis was playing piano and tenor and had become the person we could rely on to help us with the melodies to tunes and the difficult chord progressions. He had a great feel for pretty melodies and had a superb ear. He was playing piano by ear because his major instrument at Dillard was the clarinet. Eventually Harold Battiste organized us into the American Jazz Quintet.

Before Ellis's tenure in the Marine Corps, Ellis, Harold and Blackwell went to Los Angeles to "get into something." It was during the summer of 1955 when they said that it was urgent that I join them. I responded. We hung out with Ornette Coleman, which established a lifelong relationship with Ornette.

Upon our return from California, Nat took Harold's place in the American Jazz Quintet (since Harold elected to remain on the West Coast). We eventually recorded for AFO Records. I became the assistant director of the Southern University Band in 1963 and moved to Baton Rouge. I became Jazz Artist-in-Residence for the Orleans Parish Schools and eventually recommended Ellis Marsalis, Henry Butler and Bert Braud for the music faculty of the New Orleans Center for the Creative Arts (NOCCA). The rest is history.

Finally, I believe that Ellis Marsalis is one of the most important persons in twentieth-century America. His musical talent, personal sacrifices, musical family, and their international stature combined with his former students and all of us who are colleagues to emphasize my previous statement. I still enjoy listening to him play and had the pleasure of participating on a February 4, 1996, concert in which the Louisiana Philharmonic Orchestra featured his composition "Ballad for Jazz Trio and Symphony Orchestra," my "Musique d'Afrique Nouvelle Orleans" plus compositions by Roger Dickerson, Harold Battiste, Allen Toussaint and Germaine Bazzle. Ellis and I appear to be fellow travelers and it is my honor.

ROGER DICKERSON

Finally, I was successful in getting comments on Ellis from his closest friend, Roger Dickerson, composer and professor of music and choir director at Southern University–New Orleans. Dickerson is the godfather of Ellis's oldest child, Branford, and the composition instructor of the youngest Marsalis, Jason. He wrote:

I remember well our first encounter. We were attending Sunday School at Saint James A.M.E. Church on North Roman Street, near Bienville Avenue. Our discovery that we shared so many interests was immediate, immensely intense, and charged with energy. We started a dialogue that Sunday morning and we haven't stopped talking yet.

It became apparent over the years that a huge chunk of the treasure we shared was due to our being privy to all that transpired in each other's lives. Our friendship deepened during the high school and college years. In a sense, we were—each to one another—the biological brother neither had. Often I referred to him as "Selas." I was called "Dickey."

Some said that we were closer than brothers. There were times that we dressed exactly alike. During those early years, we only knew the association to be simple joy, incredible fun, shared trust, and unlimited mutual respect for each other and the ideals we shared.

It is truly becoming painfully evident to me that a friendship of a lifetime does not easily—if at all—allow itself to be placed within the short space of a few lines, trapped within the confines of a few pages. But I have promised; and so I must try.

I have been as close as anyone to Ellis and his early musical development. We were both growing up, developing as young, serious musicians in New Orleans. A couple of totally focused high energy teenagers we were. Music touched every aspect of our lives: school, church (the junior choir), and weekend gigs with a neighborhood band we organized. We were constantly involved—practicing, listening to recordings, learning tunes, jamming, talking, playing gigs, more talking. We only stopped long enough to begin repeating more of the same all over again. It was sheer joy. The breadth of our musical interest was enormous. It covered a wide range of formal concert music as well as the vast richness of vernacular idioms.

We had steady girl friends. We often double-dated, taking the ladies to the movies and other appropriate places. Our steadies were music students as well. And yes, they joined in—quite ably—on the running dialogue. Ellis was an excellent dancer. We all enjoyed dancing. But Ellis had an incredibly keen sense of timing that was exhibited in every move. He could groove, just as he did in playing music. However, we usually ended up playing for most of the dances we attended.

Ellis was already playing the B♭ clarinet when we met. He later acquired a deep interest in the tenor saxophone. After one summer of wood-shedding on his newly acquired B♭ tenor, he emerged that fall (beginning of the school year) "smoking." Immediately, Ellis began to distinguish himself as a uniquely gifted talent. But Ellis seemed always to have piano abilities, which came into full view during our later college years. We were both playing a variety of instruments. We were composing and arranging for small ensembles and combos, vocal quartets, concert band and jazz orchestra.

It was upon graduating and leaving Dillard University that clear, definite directions began to take place in our lives—a foreshadowing of much that we are doing today. I was off to graduate school at Indiana University to study music composition. Ellis, after completing a United States Marine boot camp, found himself playing piano—not tenor sax—on special television and radio broadcast programs in Southern California.

For both of us, the cocoon had begun to open. The piano would reign supreme for Ellis, while music composition would be my destiny. On returning to New Orleans from the Marine Corp and Southern California, he and Dolores Ferdinand, whom he had been seriously dating, were married. Now I had a sister.

Dolores had just completed a bachelor's degree at Grambling University. And she easily ranked among the upper tier of those beautiful ladies New Orleans had long been noted for. Dolores was an incredible cook, and she could sing. Some of Ellis's best ballads were written for her.

When Branford, their first child, was born, I was in Europe and could not be present for the christening. Naturally, I was to be the godfather. Harold Battiste was kind enough to stand in as proxy for me.

Following my serving in a U.S. Army Band (stationed in Heidelberg, Germany, and traveling throughout Europe and the Middle East), I spent three years in Vienna, Austria, as a Fulbright Fellow. When I returned to New Orleans, the Ellis Marsalis family had again increased. Wynton was the newest member.

I am not at all surprised—but always pleased—when I hear Branford and Wynton speaking out. Those guys heard a lot, believe me, early on. Indeed, they were saturated with our dialogue—at their house, at my house, on the lake front, in parks, on the swings. On and on it went, covering everything.

Looking back over the years, I have watched Ellis move through various stages of development. Without a doubt, Ellis has truly distinguished himself as a unique musician, the lyrical pianist that we know today, hailing out of the New Orleans tradition. Ellis has made a substantial contribution as a teacher. One needs only to look about the roster of young musical lions on the national and international scene to glimpse evidence of his pedagogy. The success, I suspect, lies in the fact that he serves as a model. Ellis's dedication and knowledge, particularly his sense of history, easily spills over into his relationship with students.

Following his acceptance of a faculty appointment with the New Orleans Center for the Creative Arts and subsequent move to a university endowed chair position, Ellis's career and musical development have expanded and soared to incredible heights. He is today a world class performer of the highest order and a true master teacher.

Ellis has always honored the ideals of his musical expression, of its mannerisms, of its craft. Ellis did not sell out. He has performed with scores of musicians of various persuasions, styles and genres.

Ellis is serious, always has been. His music is serious. It easily shares in that body of twentieth-century music representing America's most original gift to world art.

There are brilliant flashes of genius in Ellis's ability. He has an incredible ear. But he is capable of hearing far more than melodies, harmonies and rhythms. Ellis's ears could easily discern truth and justice. And they were tuned, as well, to respect, and compassion, and concern for his fellowman.

Ellis has managed to keep his feet on the ground. This is a particularly re-markable trait. A remarkable father, a true family man, his efforts have reaped valuable returns upon his friends and students, the New Orleans community, and on and on. Today the waves of beneficial effects are global. He has stayed the course in realizing a talent.

When any one of us can stay the course in realizing a talent, a great cul-tural dispensation is experienced by all of us. Ellis has had the fortitude and optimism to make it so. But it is not the end of the day. And Ellis and I have things yet to talk about. We are talking about the needs of students, the im-portance of our mutual commitment to the academic world, about the fu-ture of music in America, about issues at the heart of aesthetics and cultural perceptions. The dialogue continues; it is as important today as ever.

Appendix A

Discography

Title	Label	Year
Monkey Puzzle	AFO	1963
Piano Reflections	ELM	1978
Father and Sons	CBS	1982
Syndrome	ELM	1983
Homecoming	Spindletop	1985
The New Orleans Music	Rounder	1988
A Night at Snug Harbor, New Orleans	Somethin' Else	1989
Ellis Marsalis Trio	Somethin' Else	1990
Piano in E	Rounder	1991
The Classic Ellis Marsalis	AFO (reissue of Monkey Puzzle album on CD)	1991
Heart of Gold	CBS–Sony	1992
Whistle Stop	CBS–Sony	1994
Loved Ones	CBS–Sony	1995
With Courtney Pines		
The Vision's Tale	Antilles	1989
With Branford Marsalis		
Royal Garden Blues	CBS–Sony	1986
With Stephen Masakowski		
Friends	Nebula	1986
With Wynton Marsalis		
Standards Vol 3: "The Resolution of Romance"	CBS–Sony	1990
Joe Cool's Blues	CBS–Sony	1995

Title	Label	Year
With Marcus Roberts		
As Serenity Approaches	RCA Novus	1992
With Kermit Ruffins		
World on a String	Justice Records	1993
Hold On Tight	Justice Records	1996
With Wessel Anderson		
The Ways of Warm Daddy	Atlantic Jazz	1995
With Jason Marsalis		
Twelve's It	Columbia	1998
Video Projects		
The Seductress (with Wynton Marsalis)		1990
King Midas (with Yo Yo Ma)		1991
Stardust (with Harry Connick Jr.)		1992

Noel Kendrick, Richard Payne, Ellis, Harry Connick Jr., and Frank Minyard.

From left to right: Harry Connick Sr., Richard Payne, Kevin Whavers, Delfeayo Marsalis, Rodney Mack, Ellis, and Frank Minyard (in front of NOCCA, 1982).

Pianist Marsalis "making music" and posing for the photographer.

Ellis, Wynton, and Branford at Clark College in Atlanta, 1980s.

Wynton, Ellis, James Patterson, and Branford at Clark College in Atlanta, 1980s.

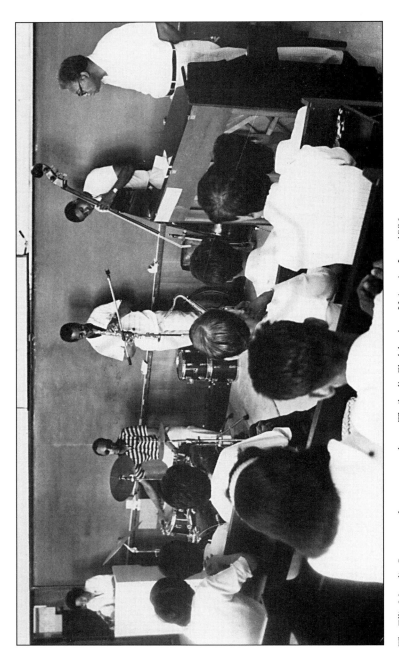

The Ellis Marsalis Quartet conducts a master class at Thailand's Chulalonghorn University, June 1986.

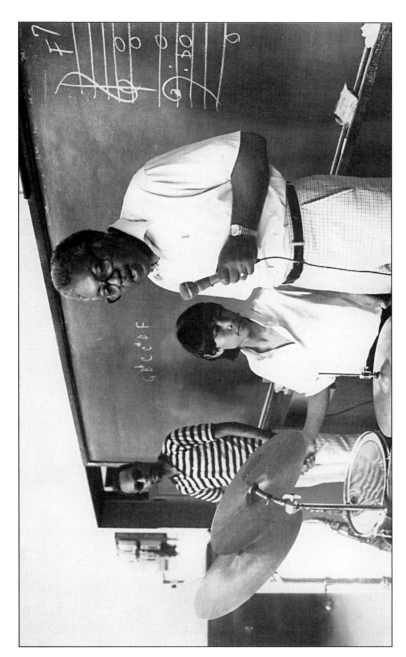

Asian tour in 1986: Noel Kendrick and Ellis with student in Bangkok, Thailand.

Professor Marsalis.

Ellis and Marcus Roberts, second from right.

During Ellis's Richmond, Va., sojourn, 1986–89.

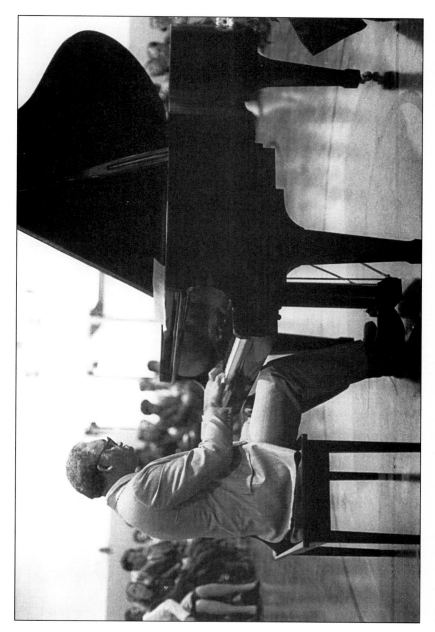

Informal concert for the community, at John B. Cary Elementary School in Richmond, Va.

Ellis Marsalis Summer Jazz Program at Indiana University of Pennsylvania.

Jason Marsalis, on drums, at the Ellis Marsalis Summer Jazz Program, Indiana University of Pennsylvania, 1992.

If Ellis can't explain it, it's unexplainable (Indiana University of Pennsylvania, 1992).

Following a Marsalis workshop at North Carolina Central University in Durham, N.C., in the late 1990s.

University of New Orleans's Big Band, spring '98.

UNO awards ceremony, 1998.

Colin Powell, former chairman of the Joint Chiefs of Staff, and Ellis exchange greetings at the Fortune 500 Forum in New Orleans, 1996.

Vocalist and guitar player Danny Barker and Ellis.

Ellis at the Bern Festival in Switzerland, receiving an award. Photograph by Michael Fichter.

Farewell concert at the Orpheum Theater in New Orleans, July 1986.

Ellis accompanies Carmen McCrae.

Yo Yo Ma, Patrick Smith, Delfeayo Marsalis, and Ellis.

Yo Yo Ma and Ellis in the studio, recording music for King Midas.

Billy Taylor, Jimmy Owens, and Ellis at an IAJE conference.

An International Association of Jazz Educators (IAJE) board meeting, from left to right: (seated) Ellis, Fred Tillis, Dennis Tini, Robert Carnow, and Bumky Green; (standing) Bill McFarlin and Chuck Iwanusa. Photograph by Michael Wilderman.

Ellis on piano, Harold Battiste on saxophone, vocalist Germaine Bazzle, David Pulphus on bass, Jason Marsalis on drums, and Delfeayo Marsalis on trombone at a concert for the Bultman Funeral Home in 1994 (courtesy New Orleans public schools' Historical Collection; Al Kennedy, photographer).

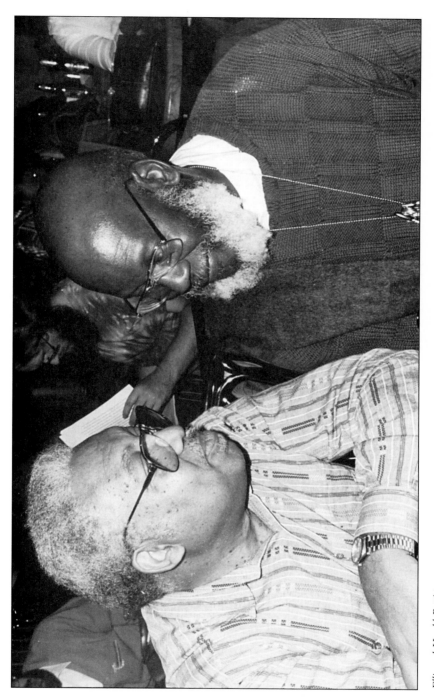

Ellis and Harold Battiste.

Benefit concert at the House of Blues in New Orleans, June 1994.

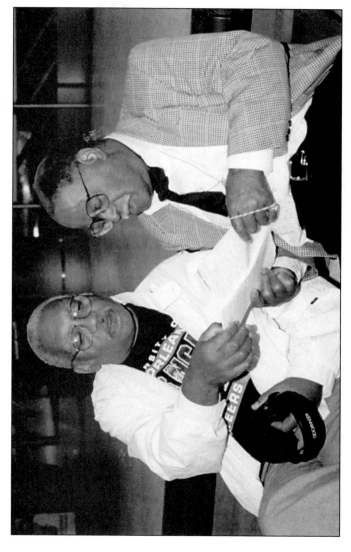

Ellis and noted trumpeter Clark Terry in Bern, Switzerland, 1997. Photo by trumpeter Joe Wilder.

Ellis and the other members of his trio, drummer Geoff Clapp and bassist Roland Guerin, backstage at Orchestra Hall in Chicago, following an appearance with the Chicago Sinfonietta. (Clapp's mother is standing next to him.)

Dolores and Ellis, a "moment of relaxation," January 1987 in Richmond, Va.

Ellis Sr. attending the wedding of grandson Delfeayo, 1997.

Dolores Marsalis celebrates her 52nd birthday, 1989.

Ellis, son Mboya, and Dr. Lorraine Wilson at the Ellis Marsalis Summer Jazz Program, Indiana University of Pennsylvania, 1992.

Ellis and son Jason.

Ellis and his oldest child, son Branford.

Ellis Marsalis at Blues Alley, D.C. Photograph by Michael Wilderman.

Appendix B

Marsalis Profundities

"I have such strong philosophies about education, it can get to be boring to listen to them."

"Each state should legislate the required arts courses and make it mandated as a requirement for graduation from high school. That would open the door to serious study. I don't see music as a separate entity. If it is going to function in the academy, it has to be under the rubric of the arts and should be respected equally along with science, math, English and history. Personally, I don't see how anyone can teach history without teaching the arts. What you get then is just dead presidents and war heroes. You leave out architecture, music and recreation."

"At the time when they're developing, they need to be exposed to activities interesting and thought provoking."

". . . Music is the greatest free enterprise activity in this country. We don't get support from anybody. The wildcats get support from the legislature in the oil business. We don't get support from anybody."

"Thinking of jazz as a field is an illlusion. Jazz is a form of free enterprise within the entertainment business."

"I'm more interested in spreading the whole (jazz) education process. The jam session, where people used to learn, is no longer a common occurrence or part of the social fabric of young players."

"[Y]ou don't really teach anybody anything. The best you can do is to find a student who's receptive to influence and discipline, and then guide and sustain him."

"If I have to choose between a strong talent and a hard worker, I'll take the hard worker every time."

"As a nation, we've allowed the pop aspects of our culture, the stuff created by television, to dominate too many elements of our lives. Too many kids have never heard of 'Oklahoma!' or 'Guys and Dolls'."

"I have very strong feelings about American music . . . I'm thinking in terms of trying to develop the means by which the younger generation and future generations can 'get at' American Music. The ensemble that is most flexible in terms of doing it at a level where students can get a hands-on approach is the rhythm section. I'm really talking about the music of Ellington, Gershwin, Cole Porter, Rogers and Hammerstein, Jerome Kern . . . these kids don't know anything about that unless by luck they happen to catch some on television."

"I like to see creativity developed across lines of disciplines—music, theater, dance and so forth . . . If I find a pianist who's interested in writing, I might say, 'Take this Shakespearian sonnet and set it to music.' Now the student may never be able to do that, but he can try and we can discuss it and see why he could or couldn't. The learning is in that experience."

"Improvising within one style or another is mainly a question of how you use your faculties. The process is the same, whether you're improvising early jazz or late jazz, or bluegrass—MUSIC!! The fundamentals are developed in classical music. There are no equivalents in jazz to the teaching materials—theory and method—found in the classics. It's necessary for students to learn the craft of their instrument and the language of music."

"I'm in it for the people who have the musical ability but just have been totally neglected [by the school system K–12]. Some people we get are already good players, but need the space and time to sharpen up what they already have."

"Jazz is an improvisation on the basis of music, which is not unlike most aspects of American life. . . . Jazz is more a reflection of the way America functions."

"We need a big league. We need the same kind of things they have in athletics. We could use that in the arts—and I prefer to say the arts as opposed to just saying music, because in order to be a successful musician, one needs to have a broader perspective than just looking at and listening to music. We have to study about the arts. We have to develop a visual awareness. We have to do sessions with creative writing teachers. We have to look at it from a standpoint of the arts as a whole."

"I believe in fundamentals . . . I think too often we leave out fundamentals and get involved in exotic activities."

"I think there's a creative side to everything we do. There are too few situations where kids can participate in that there are no right or wrong things. Not that there's anything wrong with right or wrong. We need that. But I think the best way to deal with creativity is to take the right and wrong out of it."

"At NOCCA, all of the jazz students had to take classical music, because I said so."

"One should not go into jazz with the idea that you can make a lot of money. If you believe in what you're doing, and then times get hard, and they always get hard, then you'll stick with it."

"The time will come when the term 'jazz' is dropped because it will have become totally ineffectual. It won't mean anything because we've allowed it to mean 'everything' for so long."

"If you teach music in such a way that it makes serious demands on the students, they'll begin to realize that the music is serious. Not because you're telling them it's America's contribution to world culture . . . If you treat the music as second-rate then that's the message the students are going to get."

"Classical music allowed some people to visualize it in terms of a career, . . . but as a black musician that wasn't necessarily an option of mine. It wasn't that there weren't black musicians doing that; it just wasn't that close to me. It didn't speak to me to that extent. So I gravitated more to the music of my [culture]. Jazz became the challenge."

"Most kids are inundated with pop music, which means their concentration is going to be on that. You cannot expect a kid to appreciate the great

American novel if the only thing he's been exposed to is comic books. You have to have a quality, basic education across the board."

"You have to look at the nightclub business as a business, pure and simple. Whatever is most rewarding to the people that have responsibility of keeping the club going is the thing that they're going to go for. People are going to have to develop marketing techniques to sell the music. Jazz has never had support."

"At a time when individualism is becoming an endangered species, jazz represents a celebration of the individual."

"I don't really consider myself a success; I consider myself a survivor."

"When you grew up in the South under segregation, the kinds of things the people in the mainstream think of in terms of their lives is not always open to you. The only thing that was open to most blacks at that time was working for the post office, being a school teacher or finding whichever broom or mop had your name on it. Being a musician was sometimes a psychological escape; it was also a social enjoyment . . . It wasn't cut-and-dried Wall Street view of music as a business."

"As a group of people we bought into an impossible situation where we spent too much time seeking to be *equal* and the only avenues in the South towards that kind of equality were teaching . . . and preaching."

"Educating or performing? To me it's the same, just a different audience."

"Universities function primarily from a literate culture and jazz music existed and developed in an oral culture."

"We are moving towards an American music that's going to be recognized by all Americans as their music. America is searching for a certain kind of unity which it has not achieved. And the reason it has not been achieved is because of the racism. If we overcome this attitude in all aspects of the society then we'll notice the same thing in music."

"Jazz is a music that not only has a history, but is necessary to a person's education. . . . For a professional musician, it's indispensable. And if a person is going to become a functioning, knowledgeable American citizen, they need to understand the music intelligently as a listener. . . . This is not a cloistered activity."

"Administrators too often consider music and art expendable, and any support that is given is usually too little to be of any significance."

"You learn to play jazz by listening to jazz and then by practicing, practicing, practicing. . . . If you want to earn a living playing jazz you'd better know some basic economics—what's commercially viable, how to budget through lean times, how to talk to a banker."

"You learn music like you learn a language. . . . You can learn to read and write a language, but to truly participate—to speak—you have to hear that language. You become proficient in a language by developing a vocabulary and by using it every day. You have to practice that language a lot or you don't get very good at it. It's the same process with playing music."

"There's a chance, if enough standards are laid down, that one day students will be able to approach jazz as a distinct discipline."

"As we enter the final decade (1990s) of the twentieth century, it becomes increasingly obvious that the needs of the present and future jazz performances must be met in ways other than those provided by the nightclub."

"Music educators either cannot or will not include jazz instruction as a part of their lesson plans. . . ."

Appendix C

In His Own Words

AN ESSAY ON JAZZ

A friend of mine was sharing some information he was gathering under the title of "African-American Classical Music." When I asked him about the title and what exactly was African-American classical music he replied: *"Jazz."*

I have been uncomfortable with the title "African-American classical music" as a substitute description of jazz for quite a while. There seems to be a feeling of quiet desperation attached to the title. Just below the surface is a psychological need to "legitimize" jazz music. Hence, some of us have expropriated the term *classical* in a manner of means justifying ends (or is it ends justifying means?). In a nation where revisionist history is commonplace, rumor becomes legend masquerading as truth. It serves little or no purpose to create window-dressing terminology as a substitute to describe a musical contribution as significant to American culture as jazz. Whatever feelings we have about the inadequacy of the term *jazz*, they cannot be resolved by creating an artificial substitute. However, before we embrace African-American classical music as an all-encompassing descriptive title, let's examine the definition of the term *classical*.

The electronic *American Heritage Dictionary* lists four references to define the word *classical:*

1. The style of ancient Greek and Roman art, literature, or culture.
2. Versed in studies of antiquity (i.e., ancient times).
3a. The musical style that prevailed in Europe in the late part of the eighteenth century.

3b. Concert music or *all music other than popular music and folk music.* (emphasis added)
4. Standard or traditional rather than new or experimental.

When we examine these definitions, it becomes clear immediately that each reference pertains to European culture and excludes all types of folk and popular music. There is also a very strong reference to the supremacy of the concert stage as a primary performance venue.

Those who champion the development of jazz pedagogy fully recognize the difficulty of getting America's academic community (K through terminal degrees) to acknowledge the artistic validity of jazz. We cannot expect to develop pedagogical concepts by starting with a built-in liability in the language we choose to describe this music. Since we think in words, it is necessary to establish the proper approach, through the language, to discuss the ways and means of developing the skills needed for verbal communication as well as communition through performance.

During my brief tenure as the director of the jazz studies division at the University of New Orleans, I have seen the results of sustaining an exclusively Eurocentric music curriculum in a city whose cultural milieu dictates other listening experiences. If we are to significantly educate young American music students today, there must be options to study music well beyond the concert stage and the opera house. Music educators must willingly shed the cloak of conservatism and provide the necessary leadership toward the teaching and performing of all types of American music.

In an essay in *Reconstruction*, a newly published journal, author John Gennari commented on the state of jazz in America. "When one turned to the *New York Times*," Gennari wrote, "one found an editorial distinction between 'Music' and 'Jazz/Pop'—a cultural pecking order in which the Philharmonic always and forever stands higher than The World Saxophone Quartet, in which the Juilliard String Quartet is assumed to operate at a higher level of musical expression than the Modern Jazz Quartet."[1]

This form of cultural arrogance helps to perpetuate the miseducation of music educators (current and future) and their nonmusician peers who are expected to become the ticket-buying audience. Listening to jazz as an esthetic experience is not germane to mainstream American sensibilities. Just as it is "possible for John Burks 'Dizzy' Gillespie to receive a Grammy 'Lifetime Achievement' Award," said Gennari, "it is also possible for the people who gave him the award to remain unfamiliar with any particular Gillespie recording."[2] Political correctness abounds.

A close observation of the systematic exclusion of jazz studies instruction (reflecting the oral tradition) graphically illustrates a tragic form of cultural negligence from those in positions of authority. However, there is a significant hurdle to cross when one attempts to organize the concepts of jazz improvisation into an academic discipline that must function within the framework of a traditional Eurocentric-based music curriculum. The Eurocentric-based curriculum courses that are essential to the definition (both connotative and denotative) of the American culture do not address the direct needs of the aspiring jazz performer.

RESPONSIBILITY (COMMENCEMENT ADDRESS AT CALIFORNIA STATE UNIVERSITY, NORTHRIDGE)

I would like to congratulate each one of you for maintaining the discipline and tenacity it takes to complete the process of graduating from a university. You have reached a milestone in your educational career. However, as you congratulate yourself for this significant achievement, it is also time to reflect on the responsibility that accompanies this achievement.

The *American Heritage Dictionary* defines *responsibility* as "involving personal accountability or ability to act without guidance or superior authority." It further states that one should be "capable of making moral or rational decisions on one's own and therefore answerable for one's behavior." It is the concept of responsibility I wish to share with you today.

As a youngster growing up in New Orleans and surrounded by music, I knew I loved it but I was not conscious of professsional opportunities in music. As I entered Dillard University in 1951, New Orleans was a racially segregated city and career opportunities in all areas were severely limited for American Africans. I had recently discovered the music of Charlie Parker and John Burks "Dizzy" Gillespie but, with the exception of one member, the music faculty at Dillard University was totally unsympathetic to the idea of music majors developing jazz skills. I found myself in the midst of a giant contradiction. I was a music major at a predominately black university in New Orleans, Louisiana, the birthplace of jazz, where the music faculty was singing the praises of European concert music and condemning America's only indigenous musical contribution to world culture—JAZZ.

Being two months shy of my seventeenth birthday and short on both maturity and diplomacy, I did not endear myself to my superiors at the university. While I knew something was incorrect about their negative attitudes toward the music of my heros, my youthful innocence and overly protective parents rendered me cautious to the point of timidity.

I was constantly bombarded with negative advice regarding the performance of music professionally by people who were neither performers nor patrons of my beloved jazz music. My parents said that music was too risky and suggested I get a degree in business so I would have something to fall back on. The music faculty suggested music education so I would be able to teach and have something to fall back on. A friend of my father said I should major in math because I could get a job with a math degree. He then asked what did I want to do and I replied, "I want to be a musician." He replied, "You can't make any money being a musician." When I gave the example of Capitol recording artist Nat "King" Cole as being a successful musician he retorted, "There's only one of him," to which I replied "There was only one of me." He did not bother to reply. Nevertheless, I managed to graduate four years later with a degree in music education.

After graduation I immediately made two promises to myself:

1. I would go to New York and play with the giants of the jazz world and;
2. I would never become a teacher.

Needless to say, I never kept either promise.

If we are to assess our achievement to this point we must ask ourselves two questions: (1) What do I really want to do? and (2) If I continue doing what I am doing the way I am doing it, will I achieve it?

How do you see the role your professors play in your learning process? Are your professors really here to "educate" you or is this something you alone can do? What is your responsibility to yourself in this educational process? Did you pursue a degree so you might have something to "fall back on"?

In some ways a university is like a supermarket. There are lots of items to choose but not all of them are good for you. It is your responsibility to investigate what is available and make your decisions wisely but carefully. None of us would think of going into a supermarket and pushing a basket to the manager and saying, "Tell me what to eat." However, this is precisely what we do when we enter a university: present ourselves to the professors and say, "Here I am, educate me."

If you wish to assess your current position, here are two questions you may wish to ask yourself. What do I really want to do? If I continue doing what I am doing the way I am doing it, will I achieve it? Becoming a responsible person is a lifelong challenge. We are told that success is a journey, not a destination. That journey begins with one's acceptance of countless responsibilities. These two questions will assist you in evaluating your life while helping you to focus. As you reflect on your academic experience here, try and recall as much as you can about the learning process.

What role did your professors play in your learning process? Were your professors really here to "educate" you or is this something you alone can do? What is your responsibility in this educational process? Did you pursue a degree so you might have something to "fall back on," or were you seeking a quality education?

In some ways a university is like a supermarket. There are lots of items from which to choose but you cannot take them all. It is your responsibility to investigate what is available and make your decisions carefully but wisely.

Ask yourself "Did I approach my education in this manner?" If you are in the right place, at the right time with the right equipment and the right attitude you will, without a doubt, be responsible.

The current picture for university graduates in the job market is not always cheerful. However, we live in a world of global economic opportunities and when someone says, "You are going to have a problem finding a job, remember this: every situation that is viewed as a problem is merely an opportunity in disguise.

Congratulations once again and God bless you now and in your future endeavors.

A JAZZ MUSICIAN'S WORK ETHIC

Becoming a jazz musician requires the same dedication to ideals and principles that are emphasized in the other more traditional areas of study (i.e., medicine, law, business, etc.).

However, that message is all too often lost in the imagery perpetrated by the electronic and print media. Television, newspapers, trade magazines, and supermarket tabloids consistently elevate mediocre performances with high levels of praise where a lower level of amusement is obviously the objective of many of the recipients. In a country where profit is the bottom line and fundamental music instruction in public schools is expendable, the motivation to learn jazz techniques must emanate from a need to personally express one's self in that arena. As a practicing jazz musician I feel it incumbent upon me to share some personal thoughts about the work ethic and the development of a professional philosophy.

Be patient. Seek to discover your assets and utilize them. Also, honestly recognize your liabilities so you might work toward their early demise.

Practice not for showmanship but a clear delivery of the message only honest music presents. The object of showmanship is to be seen. This practice diverts the audience's attention away from the weak skills of one who is ill prepared. If you cannot present your music without the ostentatious display of theatrics, you should evaluate your goals.

In order to speak with clarity through your instrument you must visit each note personally. While some notes may have more weight than others they are all important in the total presentation of your performance. If you are going to take the time to develop the skill of jazz improvisation, plan to use those skills courageously and honestly. Develop the courage to create along with the skill to perform. Develop productive listening skills. If listening is to be productive, your choice of music must transcend the mediocrity of popular entertainment that permeates the electronic media. If jazz is going to be the medium of expression for your creative endeavors, take the necessary time to research performances recorded by the jazz masters, especially on your instrument.

Do not allow the trade publications to define the medium for you. While these publications perform a necessary function, in the total scheme of the music business, they seldom consider aesthetic criticism as their raison d'être. Their survival largely depends upon amassing a readership that supports their advertisers.

The jazz performer must strive to stretch himself or herself. Each performance should reflect a change for the better, especially in rehearsals. Ensemble rehearsals and private practice sessions are critical to the individual growth of the developing student. This is where most of the individual progress will occur, not in public performances. Public performances contribute to personal development only when finely honed skills are on display. When the time arrives to perform publicly, the jazz musician should be willing to:

1. Share what has been learned with an audience. Help the audience to experience the quality that comes from an honest performance.
2. Evaluate his or her performance so he or she will know what to practice for continual self-improvement.
3. Purge himself or herself of the incessant temptation toward mediocrity. Very often we play a part or a solo just well enough to get by.

An enthusiastic performance usually produces an enthusiastic response just as an honest performance will produce an honest response.

4. Dress in a manner befitting the performance. Work attire sends a message to the audience reflecting the performer's attitude toward his or her presentation. The effectiveness of the performance is both aural and visual.

5. Avoid mind-altering stimulants unless medicinally prescribed. A sober mind produces a sober performance.

6. Practice punctuality. Being on time also reflects a performer's attitude about his or her performance. If it is worth performing, it is worth starting on time.

One of the definitions of success listed in the *American Heritage Dictionary* is "The achievement of something attempted." If this definition of success is to be within your grasp, I ask you to remember this principle:

Be in the *right place* at the *right time* with the *right attitude* and the *right equipment*, ready to do the job.

Notes

PREFACE

1. Telephone conversation with Ellis Marsalis III, 1 September 1996.
2. Gary Giddins, "Choices," *New York Times*, 6 June 1995, p. 6.
3. Peter Watrous, "Father of Wynton, Branford, et al. and of a Genre's Renaissance," *New York Times*, 3 June 1995, p. A17.
4. Michael Erlewine, et al., eds., "Ellis Marsalis," *All Music Guide to Jazz*, 2nd ed., San Francisco: Miller Freeman Books, p. 479.
5. Ellis's first encounter with the National Endowment for the Arts was in 1976, at which time he was the recipient of a grant in the amount of $4,000.
6. Telephone conversations with Dolores Marsalis, 1995–1998.

CHAPTER 1

1. "Growing Up in New Orleans," In *New Orleans Stories*, ed. John Miller and Genevieve Anderson, San Francisco: Chronicle Books, 1992, p. 23.
2. Richard Cook and Brian Morton, *The Penguin Guide to Jazz on CD*, New York: Penguin Books USA, 1996, p. 859.
3. Keith Spera, "Movin' Out and Movin' On with His Music," *Times Picayune* (Laginappe), 23 October 1998, pp. 8, 10. And so it is, as announced October 23, 1998, that Jason would be "moving out" of his parent's home as he "moves on" with his music. He was taking the semester off (1998–1999, fall), with plans of "finishing his degree" sometime in the future. He also terminated his affiliation with his father's trio, after seven years, with his father's complete understanding. During the summer (1998), "Twelve's It" was released by Columbia. The very appropriate billing was "The Ellis Marsalis Trio, Introducing Jason Marsalis."
4. "Newsmakers," *New Orleans*, January 1996, Vol. 30, #4, p. 59.
5. Conversation with Ellis Marsalis Jr., 14 February 1996, New Orleans.
6. Kalamu ya Salaam, "Our Music Is No Accident," *New Orleans Tribune*, July 1995, p. 8.
7. Interview with Ellis Marsalis Sr., 26 June 1997.
8. Interview with Yvette Marsalis, 26 June 1997.
9. Leonard Feather, "Bridging the Generation Gap: The Marsalis Family," *The Instrumentalist,* November 1984, p. 11.

10. Correspondence with Ellis Marsalis Jr., 5 August 1997.

11. *Ibid.*

12. *Ibid.*

13. Conversation with Ellis Marsalis Jr., 14 February 1996, New Orleans.

14. *Ibid.*

15. Geraldine Wyckoff, "Ellis Marsalis: Believing in the Music," *Jazz Times*, December 1990, p. 45.

16. "Ellis Marsalis, Patriarch of Jazz," *A Mind Is* . . . , Vol. 2, #l, Fall 1992, p. 12.

17. *Ibid.*

CHAPTER 2

1. Harold Battiste, *New Orleans Heritage, Jazz: 1956–1966*, n.d., p. 18.

2. Correspondence with Ellis Marsalis Jr., 5 April 1997.

3. *Ibid.*

4. *Ibid.*

5. Al Kennedy, *Jazz Mentors: Public School Teachers and the Musical Tradition of New Orleans*, Dissertation, University of New Orleans, 1996.

6. Conversation with Ellis Marsalis Jr., 5 August 1997.

7. Correspondence with Ellis Marsalis Jr., 5 April 1997.

8. *Ibid.*

9. Ellis Marsalis Jr., Foreword to *The Collected Piano Works of R. Nathaniel Dett*, Miami, Fla.: Summy-Birchard, Inc./Warner Brothers, 1996.

CHAPTER 3

1. Peter Gilstrap, "Limelight," *Washington Post*, 20 June 1993, p. G10.

2. Erik Philbrook and Jim Steinblatt, "This Functional Family," *ASCAP Playback* (Special Expanded Summer Issue, 1996), p. 6.

3. NPR interview with Elizabeth Perez Luna.

4. *Ibid.*

5. Don Heckman, "Swingin' in the Stacks," *Los Angeles Times*, 23 March 1996, p. F12.

6. "Jazz man's horn plays the range," *Richmond Times Dispatch*, 15 February 1987, p. L12.

7. Philbrook and Steinblatt, *op. cit.*, p. 7.

8. Peter Watrous, "Here's Branford," *New York Times Magazine*, Section 6, May 3, 1992, p. 78.

9. Communication via Delfeayo Marsalis.

10. Thomas Sancton, "Horns of Plenty," *Time*, 22 October 1990, p. 66.

11. *Ibid.*

12. *Ibid.*

13. Peter Watrous, "New York Plans to Build a Concert Hall to Jazz, the First of Its Kind," *New York Times*, 5 February 1998, p. B3.

14. Linda Kohanov, "Horn of Plenty," *CD Review*, 19 September 1981, p. 99.

15. Mitchell Seidel, "Profile: Wynton Marsalis," *Down Beat*, January 1982, p. 52.

16. Wynton Marsalis and Frank Steward, *Sweet Swing Blues: On the Road*, New York: W. W. Norton and Co., 1994, pp. 177-178.

17. *Ibid.*, 84-85.

18. *Ibid.*, 99.

19. "Wynton Marsalis Finally Teams Up with His Dad," *Times Picayune*, 3 July 1990, p. C7.

20. Telephone conversation with Wynton Marsalis, 17 September 1996.

21. *Ibid.*

22. Telephone conversation with Ellis Marsalis III, 1 September 1996.

23. Peter Gilstrap, "Limelight," *Washington Post*, 20 June 1993, p. G10.

24. Robert Frank, "Third Brother Delfeayo Marsalis is paying his own dues," *Boston Sunday Globe*, 27 August 1989, p. 76.

25. Delfeayo Marsalis, "Negroid Fatherhood."

26. Conversation with Dolores Marsalis, 26 June 1997.

27. Interview between David Swanzy and Jason Marsalis, 3 March 1998.

28. Comments made by Ellis Marsalis Jr., during WBGO broadcast, Newark, N.J., 26 April 1996.

29. Conversation with Dolores Marsalis, *op. cit.*

30. *Ibid.*

CHAPTER 4

1. Lawrence Wright, "Return of the Godfather," February 1989, *Southern Magazine*, p. 44.

2. Teresa Annan, "An 'A' for the Arts," *The Daily Break (Virginian/Ledger-Star)*, 28 September 1986, p. G3.

3. Vincent Fumar, "Marsalis Isn't Burning His Bridges," *Times Picayune—Lagniappe*, 18 July 1986, p. 1.

4. "Marsalis Leaves His Heart Behind in New Orleans," *Richmond News Leader*, 11 August 1986, p. 16.

5. Rhonda McKendall, "Jazz Patriarch Ellis Marsalis Leaving City," *Times-Picayune,* 7 June 1986, p. B1.

6. Correspondence with Dr. DePillars, 30 September 1986.

7. Ralph Adamo, "Ellis Marsalis: The Future Away from New Orleans," *Gambit*, 19 July 1986, 11–12.

8. Elizabeth Mullener, "Marsalis Will Leave, But His Heart Won't," *Times Picayune*, 10 August 1986, p. K1.

9. Clarke Bustard, "Marsalis's Tenure May Forge Musical Link for City," *Richmond Times Dispatch,* 17 August 1986, p. J2.

10. Annan, *op. cit.*

11. Bustard, *op. cit.*

12. *Ibid.*

13. Sonya Weakley, "Mentors Prove Education Benefits," *Richmond Times Dispatch*, 5 June 1988, p. T9.

14. "Marsalis Leaves His Heart . . . ," *op. cit.*

15. Harriet McLeod, "Marsalis Leaving VCU for La. Post," *Richmond News Leader,* 29 September 1988, p. A20.

16. Correspondence with Ellis Marsalis Jr., 12 December 1988.

17. Elizabeth Mullener, "Marsalis Plans to Launch UNO Jazz Project," *Times Picayune,* 29 September 1988, pp. B1–B2.

18. *Ibid.*

19. Harriet McLeod, "Marsalis Says Farewell with Standing-Room-Only Jazz Gig," *Richmond News Leader*, 11 March 1989, p. A43.

20. Elizabeth Mullener, "Marsalis Plans to Launch . . . ," *op. cit.*

APPENDIX C

1 John R. Gennari, "Jazz and the Cultural Canon," *Reconstruction*, Vol. 1, No. 3, 1991, Cambridge: New Departures, p. 25.

2. *Ibid*, p. 26.

Index

About the Author

D. Antoinette Handy (bachelor of music, New England Conservatory of Music; master of music, Northwestern University; diploma, Paris National Conservatory) is a native of New Orleans, Louisiana. A flutist, Ms. Handy spent more than twenty years as a symphony musican, both in the United States and abroad. She served as organizer, manager, and flutist with the chamber group Trio Pro Viva (specializing in the music of black composers) for three decades. Her teaching tenures include Florida A&M, Tuskagee, Jackson State, Southern (New Orleans), and Virginia State Universities. In 1971, Ms. Handy was a Ford Foundation humanities fellow at North Carolina and Duke Universities. She joined the staff at the National Endowment for the Arts in 1985 as assistant director of the music program and assumed the duties of director in 1990. Ms. Handy retired in July 1993. Also in 1993, she received an honorary doctorate in music from the Cleveland Institute of Music and delivered their commencement address. In 1997, she received an honorary doctorate from Whittier College. She is a frequent lecturer, has published articles and book reviews in numerous professional journals, and has written several books, among them *Black Conductors* (1995), also by Scarecrow Press.

Dill